*Follow the clear photographs
to install a:*
Disk Drive
Modem
Sound Card
Mouse
Printer
Game Port
Video System
Scanner
CD-ROM Drive
And More!

Programming Illustrated shows you in full color:

- What happens when a computer program runs

- How a programmer writes a Windows application

- Why a program works like it does

- How DOS, Windows, OS/2, and Mac programming differ

- What loops, clauses, and instructions are

Computers Illustrated shows you in full color:

- What happens when you turn on your PC

- How your machine loads and runs programs

- Where the information goes that you type in

- How monitors, printers, and modems work

- What goes on within the operating system

Upgrading Your PC Illustrated

Written by
Allen Wyatt

Designed by
Amy Peppler-Adams

que

UPGRADING YOUR PC ILLUSTRATED

Library of Congress Catalog No.: 94-65335

ISBN: 1-56529-666-4

97 96 95 94   4 3 2 1

Interpretation of the printing code: the rightmost double-digit number is the year of the book's printing; the rightmost single-digit number, the number of the book's printing. For example, a printing code of 94-1 shows that the first printing of the book occurred in 1994.

Publisher: David P. Ewing

Associate Publisher: Michael Miller

Publishing Director: Joseph B. Wikert

Managing Editor: Michael Cunningham

Marketing Manager: Greg Wiegand

Composed in *New Baskerville* and *MCPdigital* by Que Corporation.

Credits

Publishing Manager
Brad R. Koch

Acquisitions Editor
Brad R. Koch

Product Directors
Robin Drake
C. Kazim Haidri

Production Editor
Thomas F. Hayes

Copy Editor
Jeanne Lemen

Technical Editor
Michael Watson

Cover Designers
Amy Peppler-Adams
Dan Armstrong

Production Team
Accent Technical Communications
Cathleen Winkler
Julie Kirkendoll

Prentice Hall
Computer Publishing
Jeff Baker
Angela Bannan
Claudia Bell
Karen Dodson
Teresa Forrester
Joelynn Gifford
Jay Lesandrini
Bob LaRoche
Tim Montgomery
Dennis Sheehan
Amy L. Steed
Sue VandeWalle
Mary Beth Wakefield
Kelli Widdifield

About the Author

Allen Wyatt, a recognized expert in small computer systems, has been working in the computer and publishing industries for more than 15 years. He has written almost 30 books about all facets of working with computers — from programming to using application software to operating systems. The books he has written and worked on have helped millions of readers learn how to better use their computers.

Allen is the president of Discovery Computing Inc., a computer and publishing services company in Sundance, Wyoming. He lives with his wife and three children on a 350-acre ranch just outside of town, on the edge of the Black Hills. In his spare time he tends his animals, has fun with his family, and participates in church and community events.

Acknowledgments

Que thanks Brad Koch, Amy Peppler-Adams, Thomas Hayes, Michael Nolan, and "best boy" Mike Miller for their teamwork on this project. Que also thanks Accent Technical Communications for its assistance in getting this book done on time.

Trademark Acknowledgments

All terms mentioned in this book that are known to be trademarks or service marks have been appropriately capitalized. Que cannot attest to the accuracy of this information. Use of a term in this book should not be regarded as affecting the validity of any trademark or service mark. Trademarks indicated below were derived from various sources.

Microsoft®, MS-DOS®, and Windows are trademarks of Microsoft Corporation.

DeskJet and LaserJet are registered trademarks of Hewlett-Packard Company.

ScanMan is a registered trademark of Logitech, Inc.

ValuePoint, IBM PC, XT, AT and PS/2 are registered trademarks of International Business Machines Corp.

Intel is a registered trademark and StaisFAXtion, 80286, 80386, 80486, 80387, 387, DX, SX, 286, 386, 486, Pentium and OverDrive are trademarks of Intel, Corp.

Contents at a Glance

Table of Contents

Part II: Upgrading

PART I
Preparation

CHAPTER 1
Upgrading Basics

WHY SHOULD YOU UPGRADE?

You have a personal computer. You like it, but for some reason you're thinking that it should do more—it should be faster, or sharper, or be able to talk to other computers or play games or... well, you get the picture. You want your own computer *plus* something else.

Whatever you want, you don't want to buy a new computer, at least not right now. You want to increase the performance or the capabilities of your PC without spending a lot of money for a new computer.

In short, you want to upgrade.

Upgrading is the simple act of putting something new in, or on, your old PC. In most cases it's easy to do and doesn't cost much money—or, at least, not as much money as a new PC.

Why should you upgrade? You should upgrade if you want more performance from your current system. You should upgrade if you want features that aren't present on your current system. You should upgrade if you like to tinker around with electronic toys. You should upgrade if you want a better PC today.

How Do You Upgrade?

Upgrading is easy—especially using this book. Each procedure is fully illustrated with clear, detailed photographs, so you'll see exactly how to do things, step-by-step.

You don't have to be a technical wizard to upgrade your PC. Most upgrading requires nothing more than a few screwdrivers and a little patience. You can find all the parts you need at your local computer or consumer electronics store. Just sit down at a clean table with your PC, your parts, your tools, and this book.

It's easy to follow the illustrated steps to install a new sound card, CD-ROM drive, or modem. And if you run into problems (which happens sometimes), you'll find troubleshooting sections at the end of most procedures in this book.

WHAT SHOULD YOU UPGRADE?

There are many parts of your computer system that you can upgrade. Starting from the outside in, you can upgrade your:

Printer (page 176)

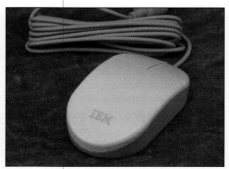

Mouse (page 156)

Keyboard (page 156)

Monitor (page 122)

Joystick (page 164)

Scanner (page 170)

Speakers (page 134)

Modem (page 144)

CD-ROM drive (page 104)

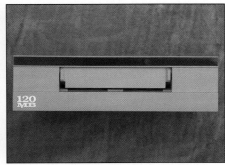

Tape drive (page 114)

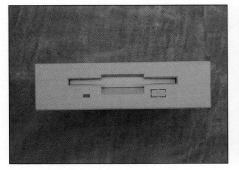

Floppy disk drive (page 84)

Hard disk drive (page 94)

Sound card (page 134)

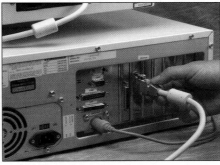

Video card (page 122)

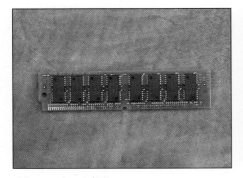

Memory (page 74)

Processor (page 64)

In short, just about anything you can unplug or unscrew, you can upgrade.

So turn the page, dust off your Phillips-head screwdriver, and let's start upgrading!

ATTE

OBSERVE
FOR H

ELECTR
SEN
DEV

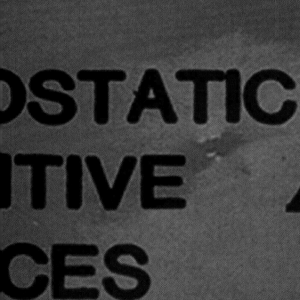

CHAPTER 2

Before You Upgrade: Taking Precautions

Tip: *Besides these files, you may wish to include any special utility programs you prefer.*

Tip: *It's a good idea to store a copy of your emergency boot disk separate from your computer. In case of a real catastrophe (fire, earthquake, etc.), your key files will still be accessible—even if your computer isn't!*

MAKING AN EMERGENCY BOOT DISK

Before you upgrade (or change any part of your system), you need to make an emergency boot disk. Since your computer can boot from either your hard disk or a disk in drive A:, you can use your emergency boot disk to start your system in case something goes wrong with your hard disk or your system files.

1 Insert a floppy disk of the proper variety (3 ½" or 5 ¼") in your A: drive.

2 Issue the format command as follows (don't forget to press Enter):

```
format a: /u /s
```

3 Wait a few minutes while the format command does its stuff.

4 When prompted, enter a volume name (optional).

5 When DOS informs you that the format is complete, indicate that you don't want another disk formatted.

6 Using the COPY command, copy the following files to the disk:

- fdisk.exe
- format.exe
- mem.exe
- msd.com
- msd.exe
- msd.ini

- recover.exe
- restore.exe
- scandisk.exe
- scandisk.ini
- undelete.exe
- unformat.exe

7 Remove the disk from the disk drive and label it "Emergency boot disk."

8 Store the emergency boot disk in a safe place, preferably away from your computer.

Your emergency boot disk should be the right size for your A: drive. This is a 3 ½" disk.

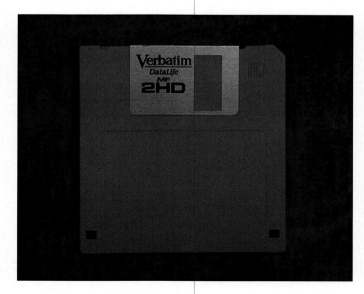

COPYING ESSENTIAL FILES TO YOUR EMERGENCY BOOT DISK

There are four main system files that control most of what you do with your computer. If these files are missing, or damaged, your computer will not start or run properly. Keeping a copy of these files separate from your hard disk is essential, just in case they are erased from your system.

- **CONFIG.SYS.** When your PC first boots up, it reads this file to discover what customization should be done to DOS. This file is located in your root directory.

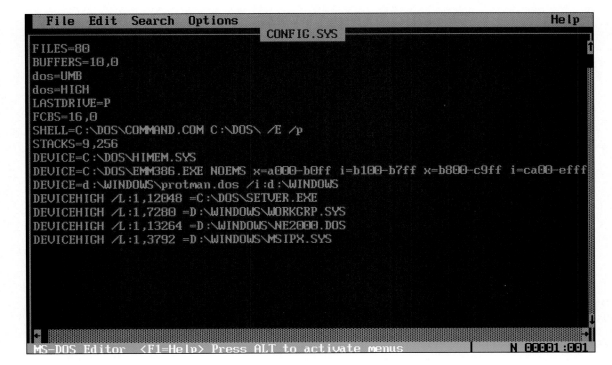

A typical CONFIG.SYS file.

- **AUTOEXEC.BAT.** This file is used to set system parameters to run DOS commands or to load standard programs. AUTOEXEC.BAT is run whenever your PC is booted, right after CONFIG.SYS is read. This file is located in your root directory.

A typical AUTOEXEC.BAT file.

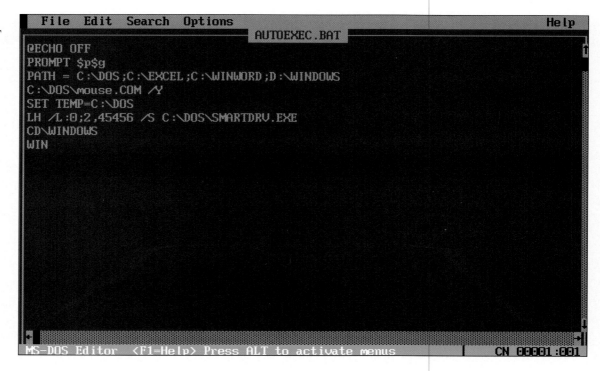

• **SYSTEM.INI and WIN.INI.** If you use Windows, these files are critical. (If you don't use Windows, you don't have these files.) They are located in your \WINDOWS directory and contain virtually every configuration parameter used to make Windows work properly.

Typical WIN.INI and SYSTEM.INI files. These files are very long; this is just the first part of the files.

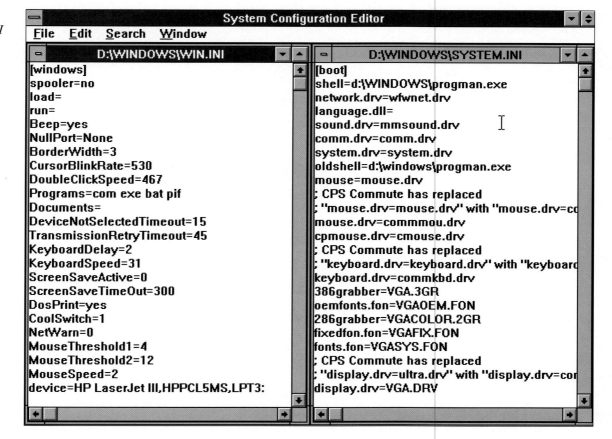

These four files should be copied onto your emergency boot disk before you begin upgrading your computer. Copying these files to the boot disk is easy—rebuilding them from scratch is not. Make sure that you recopy these files to a floppy disk every time you update any of the configuration files, or even if you just suspect they have been changed. The following steps show you how to copy these important system files to your emergency boot disk.

1 At the DOS prompt, switch to the directory where the file is located by entering one of these commands:

    CD\

or:

    CD\WINDOWS

2 After you have switched to the correct directory, enter this command:

    COPY AUTOEXEC.BAT a:

or

    COPY CONFIG.SYS a:

or

    COPY WIN.INI a:

or

    COPY SYSTEM.INI a:

This assumes you are copying these files to a disk in drive A:.

Tip: *If you have Windows, you can view, edit, and print all four of these configuration files from the SYSEDIT utility that comes with Windows. To run SYSEDIT, click on the Program Manager's **File** menu, and then click the **R**un option. Type SYSEDIT in the dialog box; then click OK.*

Tip: *Some computers have more than one hard disk drive. For example, your system may have disk drive **D:** in addition to disk drive **C:**. If Windows resides on drive **D:**, you must switch to drive **D:** before copying the files to your emergency boot disk.*

RECORDING YOUR CMOS INFORMATION

Another critical precaution to take before you upgrade is to record the information stored in your system's **CMOS**. CMOS is an acronym for complementary metal-oxide semiconductor—a type of computer chip inside your PC that contains configuration information that lets your hardware work together properly.

A modern CMOS chip.

This chip holds your computer's configuration information.

Your system's CMOS chip is battery-powered; it continues to hold information after your PC is turned off—unless, of course, the battery goes dead. If the battery goes dead, CMOS is just like any other computer memory—everything in it goes away. Because of this, it is a great idea to record the information stored in your CMOS.

1 Before you can access your CMOS information, you need to determine how to get to the CMOS information. This depends on the type of computer you have. Some computers have the setup program available in ROM, while others require a special program off a disk. Generally, the newer systems have the ROM version, while older machines use the disk method.

Watch your computer as it boots. Notice that there are several messages that appear on-screen, keeping you informed as the booting process occurs. One of the first messages may be one that describes how to access the setup program. (This message will typically occur before or during the memory check—when those numbers flip by quickly on-screen—but before accessing any drives.)

If you don't see any messages, you will need to discover what type of BIOS you have installed in your machine. This is always indicated in a message that appears when you first boot. The BIOS will typically be from a company such as IBM, Phoenix, AMI, or Award.

2 Now you need to access the CMOS information for your particular chip. Notice that the BIOS chips from different vendors use different keystrokes to access the CMOS setup routines. Try pressing the Delete key when the system is booting (during the memory check); some vendors require you to press Ctrl+Alt+S, and still others require Ctrl+Alt+Esc. If these don't work, you may need to refer to your system documentation or call the vendor where you purchased the system.

3 When the information is displayed on-screen, either write it down or press Shift+Print Screen to print it out. Put the information in a safe place so you can get it when you need it.

Tip: *If you have a PostScript laser printer hooked to your system, using the Print Screen key will not work properly. In this instance, you will need to copy the information by hand.*

BACKING UP YOUR DATA WITH DOS 6

A system backup essentially copies all the files on your hard drive to a set of floppy disks. When you back up your files, they are stored in a special *compressed format*; when you want to transfer this data back to your hard disk, you must *decompress* the data by using a special restore program.

It's a good idea to back up the data on your hard disk on a regular basis. It is especially prudent to back up this data before attempting any major upgrades to your system.

There are a number of ways you can perform a backup. With DOS 6.0 or 6.2, you can use DOS 6's improved Microsoft Backup program. To start a backup, follow these steps:

1 Enter the following at the DOS prompt:

   MSBACKUP

2 What you see next depends upon whether you have used Microsoft Backup on your system before. If you have, you will see the main backup screen and you can proceed to Step 3. If not, you will be led through a configuration process.

The main Microsoft Backup screen.

Click here to start a backup.

```
                        Microsoft Backup
   File      Help


                    ┌─ Microsoft Backup 6.0 ─┐

             ▶  Backup        ◀        Restore


                Compare                Configure


                          Quit



 Back up your hard disks and network drives
```

3 From the main backup screen, select Backup to display a set of backup parameters. Change whatever parameters necessary to perform your backup.

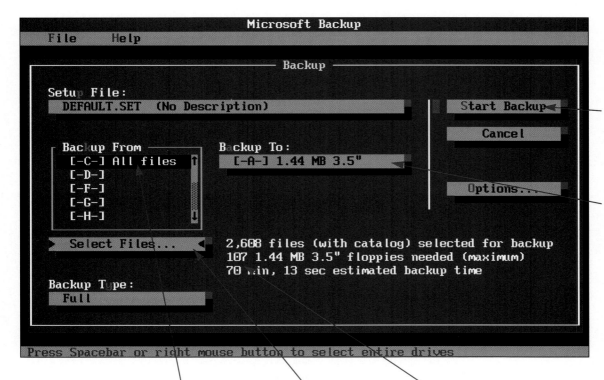

Changing the backup parameters.

Click here to start the backup with the displayed parameters.

Click here to change the disk drive to which you want to back up.

Double-click on the drive you want to back up (this selects all the files).

Click here if you want to back up individual files only.

This is the number of disk you will need for the backup.

4 Click **S**tart Backup to begin the backup. The information on your hard drive is copied to a set of floppy disks.

5 As the backup proceeds, you are asked to insert each backup disk in turn.

6 When the last disk is done, you are returned to the main Microsoft Backup screen. Select Quit to exit Microsoft Backup.

RESTORING YOUR DATA WITH DOS 6

If the data on your hard disk is lost or damaged, you need to restore the data from your set of backup disks. If you're running MS-DOS 6.0 or 6.2, you can use the Microsoft Backup program to transfer this compressed data back to your hard disk.

1 Insert the first disk from your backup set in drive A:.

2 Start the Microsoft Backup program by typing the following at the DOS prompt:

MSBACKUP

3 When you see the main Microsoft Backup screen, select Restore.

The main Microsoft Backup screen.

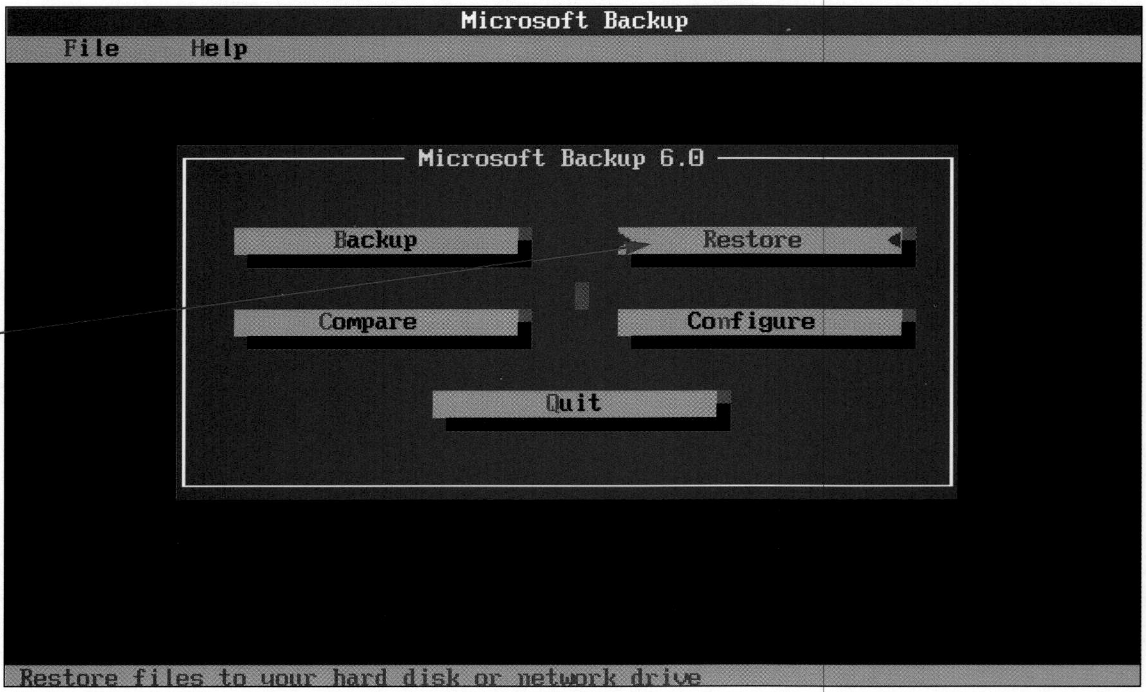

Click here to restore data you previously backed up.

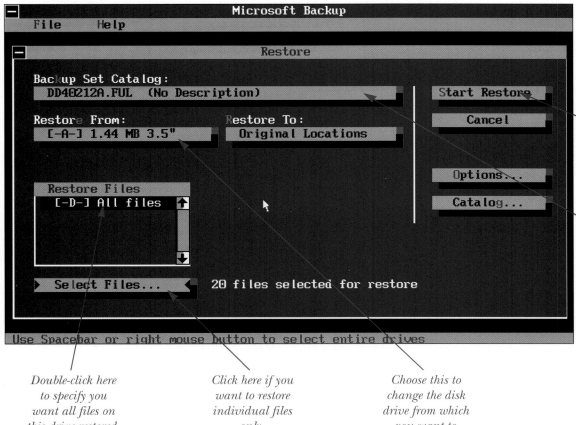

The Microsoft Backup screen after Restore has been selected.

Click here to start the restore with the displayed parameters.

Choose this area to select which backup set to use.

Double-click here to specify you want all files on this drive restored.

Click here if you want to restore individual files only.

Choose this to change the disk drive from which you want to restore.

4 To restore files you previously backed up, select what is termed a backup set (automatically created when you backed up your data) and double-click on the drive where you want the files restored.

5 Select Start Restore (available only after you've selected a backup set and the files in it). This starts the restore process.

6 The screen displays information about what is being done, how long it is taking, and what percentage is complete. If you need to swap disks, you are prompted for the disks as they are needed.

7 When the restore is complete, you are returned to the main Microsoft Backup screen. Choose Quit to exit the program.

BACKING UP YOUR DATA WITH DOS 5 (OR EARLIER)

If you have a version of DOS prior to MS-DOS 6.0, you must use the BACK-UP command to back up your data.

1 From the DOS prompt, type the following:

```
BACKUP C: A: /S
```

2 The information on your hard drive is copied to a set of floppy disks. As the backup proceeds, you are asked to insert each backup disk in turn.

RESTORING YOUR DATA WITH DOS 5 (OR EARLIER)

If you have a version of DOS prior to 6.0, you need to use the RESTORE command to transfer your data to your hard disk.

1 Insert the first disk from your backup set in drive A:.

2 Type the following command at the DOS prompt:

```
RESTORE A: C: /S/N
```

3 The data on your backup disks is now restored to your hard disk. You will need to change disks when prompted.

Tip: *Unlike the MSBACKUP utility discussed above, this older version requires you to FORMAT every disk to be used during the backup before you begin. If you run out of disks, you need to start the process over again. Also, this older version of BACKUP doesn't compress the data during backup—requiring up to twice as many disks as the newer MSBACKUP utility found in DOS 6.0 or greater.*

CHAPTER 3
Opening Up Your PC

ASSEMBLING YOUR UPGRADING TOOLKIT

You will need some selected tools with which to work on your PC. These tools are necessary for both taking the PC apart and putting it together.

The first tool you will need is a Phillips-head screwdriver, because most PCs are put together with Phillips-head screws. For most jobs, a #2 (medium-sized) Phillips-head screwdriver will do perfectly.

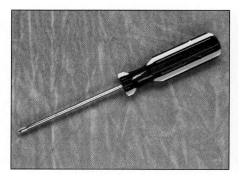

A typical Phillips-head screwdriver.

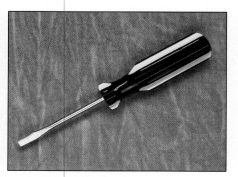

A typical flat-blade screwdriver.

Tip: *If you think you will be working on your PC system quite a bit, invest in a small cordless screwdriver that has a decent torque. They may cost a bit of money, but they can be a great time saver!*

The other thing you will find indispensable is a small flat-blade screwdriver. The blade is typically about an eighth of an inch wide.

These two screwdrivers are the minimum toolkit that you need. There are other tools that you may also find helpful, but they are not absolutely necessary. If you feel an overwhelming urge to be well-stocked, you can make a quick trip to your local computer store and pick up an all-in-one toolkit that contains all the tools you could ever remotely need when working on your computer.

A typical computer toolkit.

Toolkits such as these generally include not only a couple of screwdrivers, but also nut drivers, tweezers, and chip pullers. These kits are low cost, many times under $20. If you plan to do any repeated repairs, they are a great investment.

There is one other item that you may find helpful that is not typically included in basic toolkits—a small pair of needle-nose pliers. The type you use to work on your car are much too large. You need the smallest pair you can find; the type with a really fine nose on them. Again, these can be found at a well-stocked hardware store or in an electronics store.

SAFETY PRECAUTIONS

 Notice the order in which you perform operations. Noting where parts came from and what happened when can save you time and frustration later.

 Remove any disks from disk drives before you go poking around in the machine. Many tools carry a magnetic charge that could damage data on floppy disks.

 Don't remove any labels on the chips in your computer. Some of them (particularly those that are squarely on the top of the chips) may protect the programming on the chip from ultraviolet light, which may erase it.

 Unplug any computer components that you work on. This removes the possibility of either shorting out any components or electrocuting yourself.

 Before touching computer chips or circuit boards in a dry climate, make sure you ground yourself. (Touch some metal furniture or a coworker first.) Static electricity can really hurt sensitive electronic devices.

REMOVING CABLES

The first step in taking your computer apart is to remove the cables that are used to connect all the pieces. Remove only external cables; the internal ones always come later.

There can be any number of cables attached to the back of your computer system. In some instances, there are even one or two attached to the front. Take a look at them; if you have to move the PC so you can see where the cables connect, then do so. Note the different colors, shapes, sizes, and lengths of the cables. Notice that each of them has a different type of connector on the ends. As you become familiar with the cables, you will start to feel comfortable disconnecting and reconnecting them.

1 The first cable you should remove is the power cord (note the preceding safety precautions). If you remove the power, you remove a big potential hazard. The power cord is generally easy to identify—simply start at the wall and follow the cord back to where it is connected to your PC. This connection will be right where your power supply is located. Pull the plug out from the PC and from the wall; put it in an out-of-the-way place. (Put all your cords and cables in the same place. They are easier to find and won't get in the way.)

How to disconnect your PC's power.

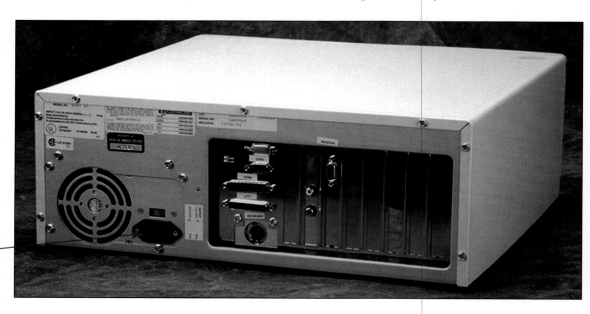

Disconnect power cord from here.

2 After the power cord is removed, you can start to remove any other cables—in virtually any order you desire. Some cables are fastened with thumb screws, and others with regular screws. Again, try to remember where they came from. Notice that most of the cables have plugs that can fit only one connector on your PC; this will help you reconnect the cables later.

Connector that fastens with thumb screws.

Some cable connectors may have thumb screws which need to be loosened.

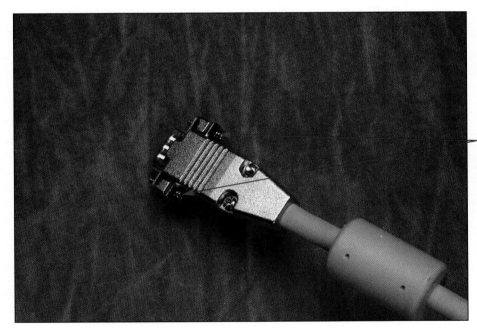

Connector that fastens with screws.

Some cable connectors may have actual screws which need to be loosened. Use the small screwdriver for this purpose.

CAUTION: Don't force the cable out of your PC by yanking on it. Most cables should disconnect easily and pull right off. If you feel as if you are forcing the cable, stop. Examine the connector to see if there are any screws that need to be loosened.

REMOVING COVERS ATTACHED WITH SCREWS

Once all the cables are disconnected, it is time to take the cover off your computer. Different types of PCs use different methods to attach their covers. The most typical method is screwing the cover on.

> **NOTE:** Computers come in many different shapes and sizes. The two most common, however, are the horizontal and vertical orientation. The horizontal orientation is often called a desktop model, while the vertical orientation is referred to as a tower model.

An example of a desktop model for a computer case.

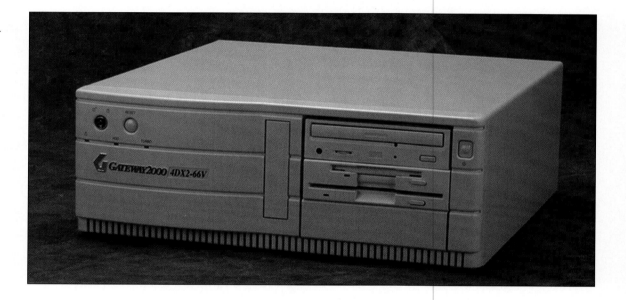

Taking the cover off your computer is a simple task and one that you'll repeat every time you upgrade your computer. Before you begin, make certain you are working on a sturdy surface and have moved any beverages out of the way so they don't get knocked over and spill on your computer. The following steps guide you through removing your computer's cover:

1 Once all the cables are disconnected, turn your computer around and find the screws located at the back of the computer case.

2 Use either the Phillips-head screwdriver or the appropriate nut driver to remove these screws. Make sure you don't lose them; they are typically a different size than the other screws used within the PC (although they may seem the same to the naked eye).

Screw locations on a PC case.

Remove only the screws that hold down the lip of the cover.

CAUTION: There are typically five to seven screws holding a cover on; these are located around the outside of the case. The screws that are located close to the fan outlet hold the power supply to the inside of the case—do not loosen these screws.

3 Once the screws are removed, stand behind the PC and place a hand on each side of the case. Slide the case backward; you may have to jiggle it a bit or try a quick, forceful jerk to get it to budge. (If you feel the urge to use a pry bar, you had better check the retaining screws; you may not have gotten them all.)

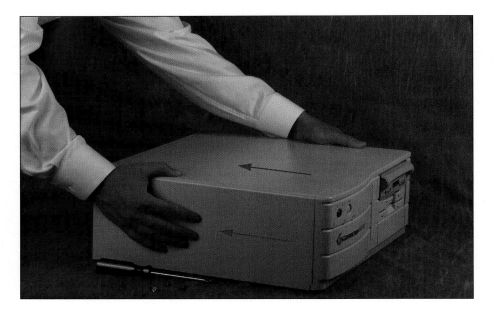

Starting to take off the case of your PC.

Tip: *Some PCs have cases that slide off from the front, rather than the back. If you have one of these computers, remember to pull the case forward from the front panel, instead of backward.*

 As the case starts to slide backward, lift the front of the case upward. It should come free fairly easily. Place the case to the side of your work area.

> **CAUTION:** Many computer cases, especially those modeled after the IBM AT, have brackets on the inside of the case that can snag cables inside the computer. Work slowly and carefully when removing a cover to avoid accidentally disconnecting any cables.

Actually removing the PC case.

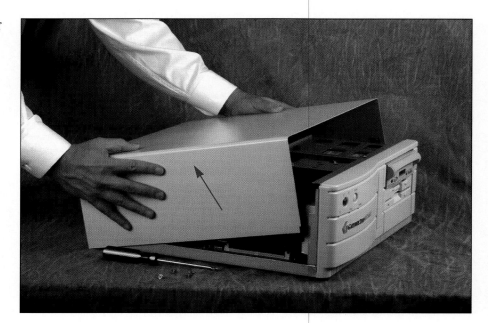

> **NOTE:** The covers on some computer cases may need to slide completely clear of the rest of the case before they can be lifted; this is because of small guide rails at the bottom of the cover and case.

REMOVING COVERS SECURED IN OTHER WAYS

Some covers do not use screws to hold them to the main part of the case. Recent models of the IBM PC such as the IBM PS/Valuepoint) don't use screws at all. Instead, you can press a button and remove the cover.

The case release latch on the IBM PS/Valuepoint.

Press here to release the cover latch.

1 Press the button on the front of the computer case.

2 Once the button is depressed, slide the cover back and remove it as described in the previous section.

Tip: *Another thing that commonly interferes with removing covers is a sort of locking mechanism. Look for a lock on the front of the PC; if there is one visible, make sure it is unlocked. Some of these locks are used for only the case, while others lock both the case and the keyboard (to keep it from working).*

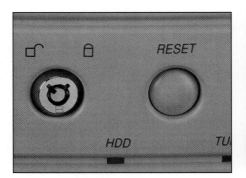

The case on this PC is unlocked.

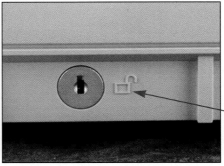

The case on this PC has been locked and cannot be removed.

Turn the lock to this symbol to unlock the case.

PUTTING THE COVER BACK ON

Tip: *Before replacing the cover, take one last look around the inside of your computer case. Make sure you didn't leave any loose wires in the way, and that all loose pieces have been removed or secured.*

If you paid attention to how you took your computer apart, putting it back together is a snap. Basically, all you do is reverse your steps.

To put your computer back together, follow these steps:

1 Put the cover on first, making sure it slides securely onto the computer case.

2 If applicable, secure the cover with the same screws you removed to take off the cover.

3 Attach any cables you previously disconnected from the back of your computer.

4 Attach the power cord to both the computer and the wall outlet.

Plugging in the PC power.

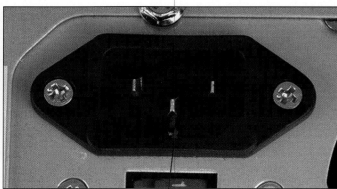

This plug...   *...goes in this socket.*

TESTING YOUR SYSTEM

Turn on your computer and attempt to start it up as you normally would. Before you begin any important work, however, you should fully test everything related to whatever you fixed or upgraded. Give it a thorough workout while what you did is still fresh in your mind.

If your computer does not work properly, don't despair. You can retrace your steps to determine if the fix or upgrade was done correctly. The biggest problems are often caused by the smallest of things. Take your time and go over everything carefully. Make sure all the connections are correct and secure; these often are a source of trouble. If worse comes to worst, you can always enlist the help of a qualified computer technician.

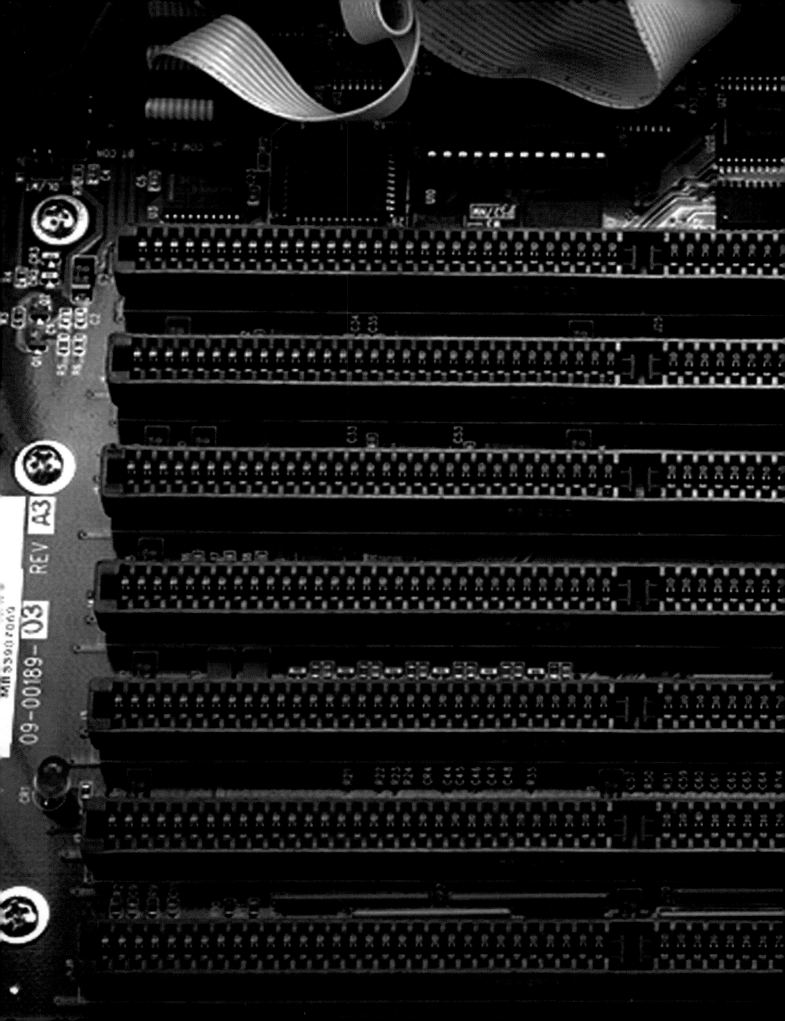

CHAPTER 4
Inside Your PC

IDENTIFYING PARTS OF YOUR SYSTEM

Typically, the largest component in the computer case is the PC power supply. This is in a self-contained box and has a bunch of red, black, and yellow wires running out of it. You probably shouldn't fool around with the inside of the power supply; it can give you quite a nasty shock if you don't know what you're doing!

A typical PC power supply.

The PC power supply should be clearly marked.

At the front of the computer case should be drive bays, disk drives, and possibly other items such as tape drives and CD-ROMs.

Drive bays on a desktop PC case.

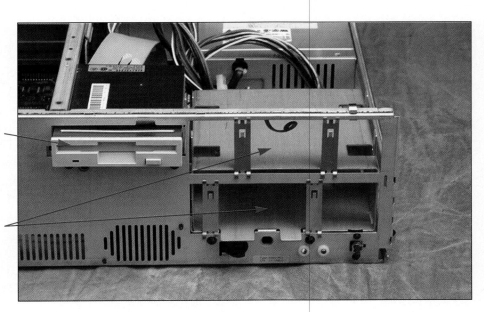

A drive bay with a disk drive in it.

These drive bays are empty and can be used for future expansion.

The largest electrical circuit board in the computer case is what is called the **motherboard**. This contains all the circuits that define the major part of the computer. You can always identify the motherboard because every other part of the computer is connected to it in some way or another.

If you see any large slots on the motherboard, these are for expansion purposes. Some of these expansion slots may already have adapter cards in them.

Expansion slots on a PC motherboard.

Empty expansion slots.

Memory, which is where your computer stores temporary information, also is another important part of your PC.

Memory modules in a modern PC.

This is a bank of memory.

These memory module slots are for future expansion.

WHAT NOT TO FIX

You need to know, right up front, that there are a few things that can be upgraded, but shouldn't be *fixed*. By and large, these are items that are either easier (and often cheaper) to replace than to fix, or items that can be hazardous to your health if you try to fix them.

First, don't fix the monitor. Inside that unassuming case is an accident waiting to happen. The capacitors inside a monitor can maintain a hazardous electrical charge for hours. Touch one and you may get a quick trip to the other side of the room—or the emergency room.

Second, don't fix the PC's power supply. Besides the fact there are typically no screws you can undo to open the power supply, there also are slow-discharge capacitors in here. Touch one of these and you'll wish you had fooled with the monitor instead.

Finally, it probably isn't worth fixing a bad keyboard. Pull that cover off and you will wonder how they ever got all those keys, springs, clips, and parts to stay inside in the first place. With the price of keyboards these days (many under $50), it is better just to bypass the hassle of fixing them and get a new one.

UNDERSTANDING ADAPTER CARDS

To enable your computer to work with various devices (such as disk drives, printers, modems, etc.), manufacturers provide various **adapter cards**. These cards allow your computer to control and communicate with the various devices.

> **NOTE:** Adapter cards are known by many different names. One vendor may refer to them as interface cards, another as controllers, another as cards, another as adapters, and yet another as boards (as in *sound board*). Any of these names can be used interchangeably.

There are several different types of adapter cards on the market, each interfacing with your computer in a different way. This is determined by the type of **bus** in your system and the type of **slots** you have available. There are three major types of buses available: ISA, EISA, and MCA. There also are two relative newcomers, VESA or Local Bus, used predominantly for video adapters, and PCI, which is a new high-performance bus design used primarily with Intel Pentium-based computers.

The following table contains information about each different type of bus:

Bus types

Type:	Stands for:	Typically found in:	Comments:
ISA	Industry Standard Architecture	Most IBM-compatible PCs	The oldest type of bus, very common.
EISA	Extended Industry Standard Architecture	High-end systems	Very fast, easy-to-use, but not compatible with ISA cards. Not very common.
MCA	Micro Channel Architecture	IBM PS/2 systems	Only used in IBM systems. Not very common.
VESA	Video Electronics Standards Association (also known as "local bus")	Newer systems	Becoming more common, especially for video cards.
PCI	Peripheral Component Interconnect	Intel Pentium-based computers	Faster than VESA in systems that take advantage of its capabilities.

When you're looking at cards and buses, you also have to keep in mind the width of the data path, typically measured in **bits**. You will find 8-bit cards, 16-bit cards, and even 32-bit cards. The width of the data path becomes critical when you are working with faster processors. If you use adapter cards that have smaller data paths than your processor, you can slow down the overall processing speed of your system.

8-bit adapter cards have only a single connector across the bottom.

16-bit adapter cards have a double connector across the bottom.

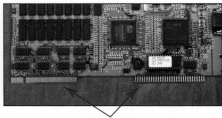

A local bus card has two widely spaced edge connectors.

SETTING UP AN ADAPTER CARD

STANDARD PC IRQ SETTINGS

IRQ	Purpose
0	System timer
1	Keyboard controller
2	Cascade to second IRQ controller (8 through 15)
3	Serial port 2 (COM2:), Serial port 4 (COM4:)
4	Serial port 1 (COM1:), Serial port 3 (COM3:)
5	Parallel port 2 (LPT2:)
6	Floppy disk controller
7	Parallel port 1 (LPT1:)
8	Real-time clock
9	Unused
10	Unused
11	Unused
12	Motherboard mouse port
13	Math coprocessor (NPU)
14	Hard disk controller
15	Unused

STANDARD PC DMA CHANNEL ASSIGNMENTS

Channel	Purpose
0	Unused
1	Unused
2	Floppy disk controller
3	Unused
4	First DMA controller
5	Unused
6	Unused
7	Unused

Before you install a new card, you have to set it up. The first rule of setting up your adapter card is to read the manual. You should pay particular attention to how the adapter card addresses memory, how it handles interrupts, and whether it uses any DMA channels.

Most adapter cards are fairly easy to install. Adding an adapter card gets more complicated if the computer already has a lot of options installed. The following list provides an overview of the configuration options you may encounter when setting up a new adapter card:

- **Memory.** Memory is used by your adapter cards to both store and transfer information. Some adapter cards use memory already within your system (part of your RAM), while others include their own memory and use a part of yours. Besides storage needs, most adapter cards use a memory address in order to communicate with the card. In the manuals for some adapter cards, these are called I/O (input/output) port addresses or a base address.

- **IRQs.** Most devices communicate with your PC through a series of *interrupts*. This means each device simply makes a signal when it needs attention by the CPU. If no signal (interrupt) is ever made, then the device is never paid attention to. Interrupts are identified through a series of IRQs, which stands for *interrupt request*. When a device is assigned an IRQ, it means that it can use the interrupt line associated with the IRQ to send its signal for attention. No two devices on your system should have the same IRQ. If they do, then the CPU has no idea which device on the interrupt line issued the IRQ. The result is unreliable system operation.

- **DMA Channels.** Some adapter cards use a high-performance data transfer technique that relies on the use of DMA channels. DMA stands for *direct memory access,* a method of transferring blocks of memory directly from the device to your PC. If the device uses DMA techniques (many disk controllers, audio cards, and other devices use DMA), it will use one of the DMA controller channels within your PC. There is only a limited number of these channels, and if you have two adapters trying to use the same channel you will run into problems.

Different adapter cards allow you to set up the card in different ways. Typically, you need to set them up through a series of jumpers or switch settings. (Jumpers are nothing but small connectors between two pins on your adapter card.)

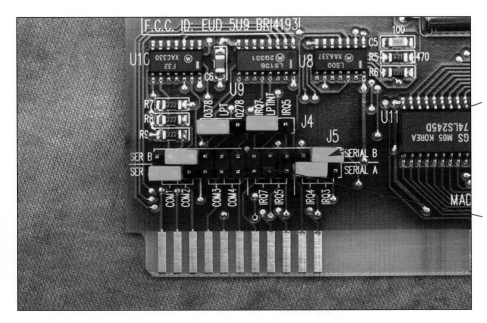

An example of jumpers on an adapter card.

— These are jumpers used to connect pins together.

— These are pins.

If the adapter card manufacturer was thinking ahead, there will be some sort of markings on the board itself to indicate what the jumpers are for. Very often, however, this is not the case, which means you need to rely on the manufacturer's documentation.

Switches come in a variety of shapes and sizes. In general there are two types—rocker and slide. As their names imply, rocker switches rock back and forth, while slide switches slide. Each switch can be turned on or off. On some switches the possible settings are 0 and 1. In these instances, 0 is the same as off and 1 is the same as on.

These switches are on. *These switches are off.*

These switches are on. *These switches are off.*

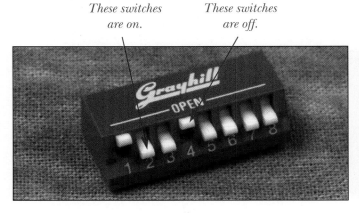

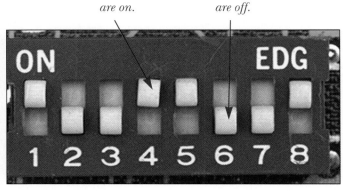

A rocker type switch.

A slider type switch.

REMOVING AN ADAPTER CARD

1 Begin by identifying the card you wish to remove. Adapter cards fit snugly within slots in your motherboard. These slots can either be on the motherboard itself or on a card attached to the motherboard.

An example of adapter card slots on the mother-board.

The adapter card is seated firmly in the slot.

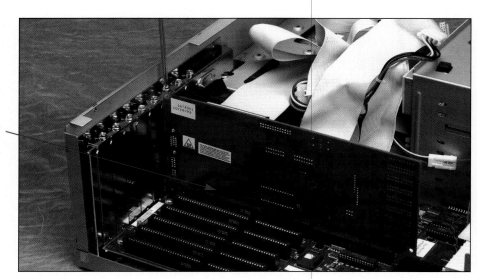

An example of adapter card slots on the IBM PS/Valuepoint.

These adapter slots are mounted vertically on a backpane.

2 Next, you need to remove all the cables attached to the exterior of the card.

3 Now you can remove the adapter card. Begin by unscrewing the retaining screw, which holds the back of the adapter card to the computer case.

4 Using both hands, grasp the adapter card near both the front and back of the card. Gently lift the card out of the computer case. There is a good chance the card will not want to come out easily. In this case, lightly rock the card back and forth from front to rear. Doing so will help to loosen the grip of the slot on the card itself.

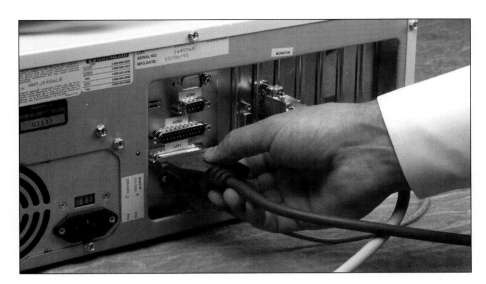

Removing exterior cables.

A secured adapter card.

Unscrew this retaining screw.

Lifting an adapter card out of the case.

INSTALLING AN ADAPTER CARD

1 To put an adapter card in your PC, first locate the proper type of slot for the type of edge connector on your card.

> **NOTE:** You can place an 8-bit adapter card in either a 16-bit or 32-bit slot. Likewise, you can place a 16-bit card in a 32-bit slot.

Removing a slot cover.

2 If there is a slot cover at the rear of the computer case, where the external part of the adapter card will be situated, remove the cover.

Sliding an adapter card into its slot.

Tip: *All adapter cards have slot covers built into them. Even though you don't need it right now, you should save your old slot cover.*

3 Slide the adapter card straight down into the slot. The rear of the adapter card should slide into the slot at the rear of the computer case, and the edge connector should seat firmly in the slot on the motherboard. You may need to apply a bit of downward pressure to firmly seat the adapter card.

*Fastening the
retaining screw.*

4 Once the card is fully seated within the adapter card slot, replace the retaining screw so it secures the adapter card in place.

This is for pin 1.

*These connectors are intended
for specific types of cables.*

A typical adapter card cable connector.   *An example of external adapter card connections.*

5 Now you need to connect the card to your computer. Adapter cards will generally have two places you can make connections. The first is internal, and the second is external. Internal connections are typically made through cable connectors on the card itself.

6 The other type of card connection (those that are external) are used to connect with devices outside your computer. There are many different types of connections in this category; connections are typically made to the part of the card that extends out the back of your system unit.

CABLE ALIGNMENT

As you are connecting internal cards, it is often easy to confuse how the cable should be attached. If you are connecting a flat ribbon cable, take a look at it. Notice how there is one edge of the cable that has a stripe. It may be red or blue or some other color, but there is a definite stripe. This marks which wire of the cable is attached to pin 1.

A typical connector cable.

This marks the wire connected to pin 1.

Orientation notch.

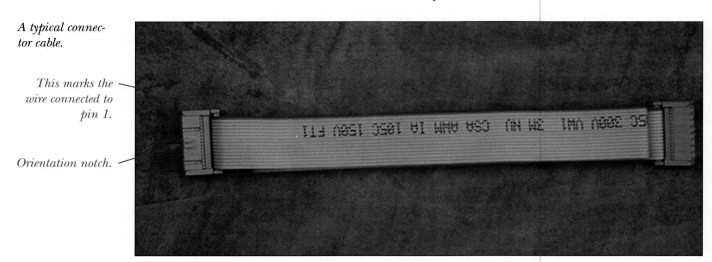

Now look at the cable connector. Somewhere near one corner of the connector should be an indication of which pin is pin 1. Orient the cable and plug so that the colored stripe is at the same end of the connector as pin 1. Your cable and connector are now properly aligned.

Tip: *Some cables may not have a red stripe or a key system. Another way to determine how to insert a cable is to align the orientation notches. Some computers have a central notch, others have dual notches. These notches may or may not prevent you from inserting the cable, but they do orient the cable correctly.*

Other cables may utilize a keyed connector. These cables have a connector with one of the holes plugged. The corresponding male connector will usually have one pin missing. Align the plugged hole on the cable with the missing pin and press the cable into place.

PART II
Upgrading

MONITOR

CHAPTER 5
System Ports

UNDERSTANDING PORTS

Input/output ports enable your PC to communicate with a wide variety of external devices such as printers, modems, mice, plotters, bar code readers, networks, and tape drives. There are three basic types of ports: parallel ports, serial ports, and game ports. This section deals exclusively with parallel and serial ports; game ports are discussed later in this book.

Parallel Ports

Parallel ports are general-purpose interfaces for your PC that can be used to transmit an entire byte at one time. Eight of the wires used in the connection are used for data—one wire for each of the eight bits in a byte. Because of this mode of transmitting information, parallel ports are generally much faster than serial ports.

A parallel port on a PC.

The parallel port.

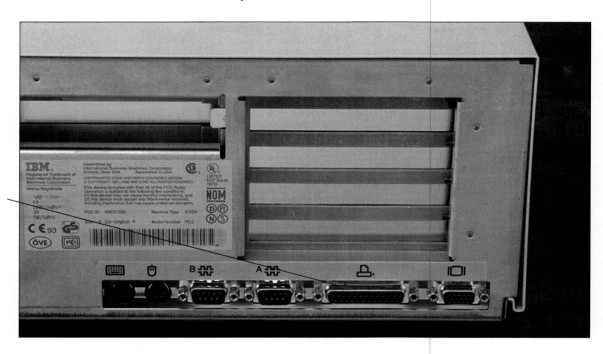

Some PCs label the port with an icon of a printer. Other PCs label them with the name of the port, which is always the letters LPT (for line printer) followed by a number designating the port number. Thus, the first parallel port would be LPT1, the second LPT2, etc. However, it is not uncommon for parallel port connectors to be unlabeled. A parallel port is the female 25-pin connector on the back of the PC.

The cables used to connect a parallel port on your PC to an external device typically contain all 25 wires. The cable connector that connects to the PC is a male 25-pin connector.

At the other end of the cable, the connector is determined by the maker of the external device. Typically, if the device is a printer, the connector is a Centronics parallel connector.

The PC end of a parallel cable.

A cable with a Centronics parallel connector.

NOTE: One of the chief drawbacks to using parallel ports is that they cannot communicate over long distances without using some sort of powered signal amplifier. Thus, most parallel cables are relatively short, measuring less than 20 or 25 feet in length. At longer distances, you may experience signal loss that makes the signal unusable.

Serial Ports

There are two fundamental differences between the original PC parallel port and a serial port. First of all, serial ports are bi-directional in nature. Secondly, a serial port transmits data only one bit at a time. This means that only one data transmission wire is needed for the interface (as opposed to eight for a parallel port), although additional wires may be defined for control purposes.

How does a device that is hooked up to a serial communications link know which byte a bit belongs to? Simple. The communications protocol used in any serial port specifies that each byte transferred must be framed (surrounded) by control bits that define where the byte starts and stops.

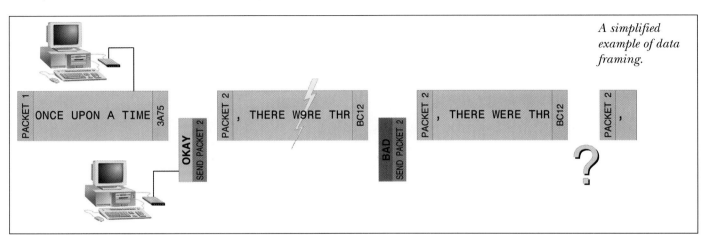

A simplified example of data framing.

When the receiving end of the serial link starts detecting bits on the line, it knows that the first bit received is a start bit. The start bit signals the device to wake up and start paying attention to what is coming in. The next eight bits are data, and the final bits are used for rudimentary error correction and to finish out the data packet.

If you take a look at the back of your PC, you see that there are either one or two serial ports (also referred to as COM ports).

Serial ports on a typical PC.

A 9-pin serial port.

A 25-pin serial port.

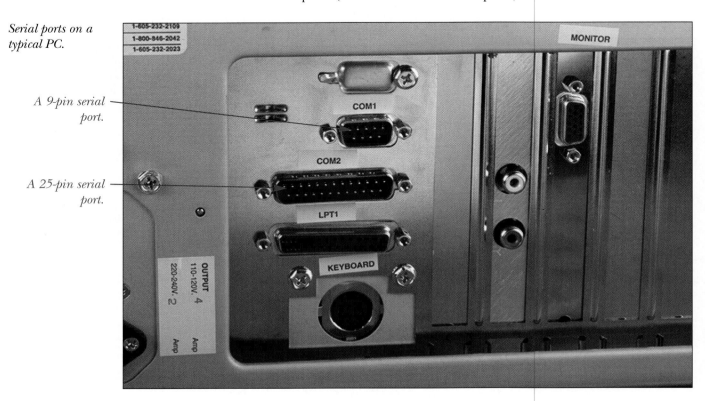

Tip: *Don't confuse the 25-pin serial port with the 25-pin parallel port. On a PC, the serial port uses a male connector, while the connector for the parallel port is female.*

Notice that there are often two types of serial connectors on a PC. While some systems may have serial ports that use the same connectors (both 9-pin or both 25-pin), many do not. The only thing that is different about the ports is that they have different connectors, otherwise they function exactly the same. You can use either port you desire.

CHOOSING PORTS

Now that you know something about parallel and serial ports, you are ready to choose the card you want to use for your upgrade. When it comes to serial and parallel ports, there seems to be a million different ways you can go. Following are the major configurations you may consider:

- **Alone.** If you search, you can usually find either a single parallel or single serial card. These are typically used if you want to expand the number of ports in your system. For instance, you may already have a parallel port and two serial ports, and you want to add another parallel port (LPT2).

- **Combined with each other.** You can easily find cards that have two serial ports and a parallel port on the same card. These cards are similar to the multi-function I/O cards discussed next, but don't provide all the features. They typically are plugged in a slot, and then a cable is connected that takes up one of the access slots at the back of the PC for the extra ports.

- **A multi-function I/O card.** If you take the previous type of card and start adding other features (such as a game port), you have a multi-function I/O card.

- **Combined with a video card.** These are not as common as they once were, but can still be found. In the early days of PCs, you would purchase the video adapter and a parallel port was included on the card.

- **Combined with a disk controller.** Some of the newer IDE controllers have I/O ports built into them. You can now find one card that controls your hard drives and floppy drives, and provides two serial ports, one parallel port, and a game port. Wow! All out of one slot!

> The exact type of interface card you select should reflect what you want to do with the ports. For instance, if you only want to add a single parallel port, you should do so. If, on the other hand, you want to upgrade your entire system, look for one of the combined I/O cards that provides all the functions you need.

Connector for external serial connector.　*A 9-pin serial port.*　*A 25-pin parallel port.*

A 25-pin serial port.　*Connects to the I/O card.*

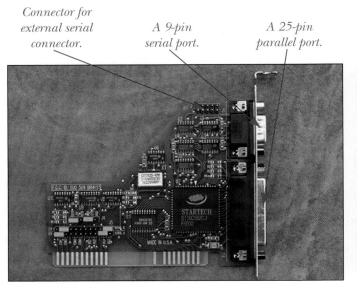

An I/O card containing two serial ports and a parallel port.

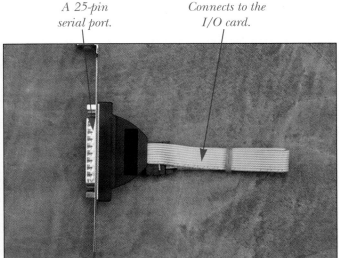

An external connector for the I/O card.

REMOVING OBSOLETE PORTS

The first step in upgrading your ports is to remove your old ones. Unfortunately, with some systems an upgrade is not possible.

In today's market, there are PC models not nearly as modular as others. For instance, take a look at the back of the IBM PS/Valuepoint. Notice that all of the ports are lined up along the bottom of the computer case. This is because they are actually built into the motherboard.

The port connectors on an IBM PS/Valuepoint.

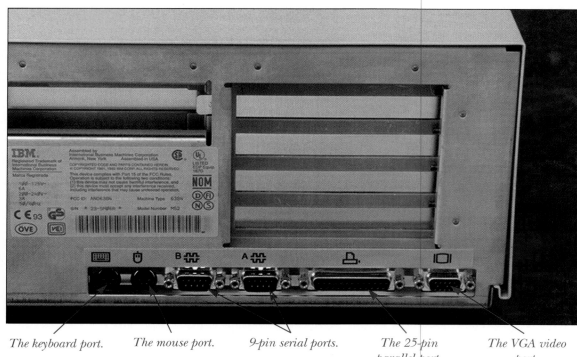

The keyboard port.   *The mouse port.*   *9-pin serial ports.*   *The 25-pin parallel port.*   *The VGA video port.*

What this means is that you cannot yank out the old ports and replace them with something new. While this may not be a big problem today, it could present tough decisions down the road if you decide you want to use a different type of serial chip. In such a case, you are locked into getting a new PC.

If you can remove your ports, however, you should follow these steps:

1 Begin by identifying which card controls the ports. This is usually done by opening your computer case and finding the serial or parallel connectors on the back of your PC. Then follow the cables from these connectors back to one of the circuit boards.

Tip: *Before you remove the circuit card that controls your ports, make sure it does not also control other parts of your system that you need to leave intact.*

2 Disconnect any cables connected to the back of the circuit card, and then remove the adapter card.

ADDING PORTS

1 Locate the slot for the new adapter card.

Removing a slot cover.

2 If there is a slot cover at the rear of the computer case, (where the external part of the adapter card is situated), remove the cover.

Sliding an adapter card into its slot.

3 Slide the adapter card straight down into the slot. The rear of the adapter card should slide into the slot at the rear of the computer case, and the edge connector should seat firmly in the slot on the motherboard. You may need to apply a bit of downward pressure to firmly seat the adapter card.

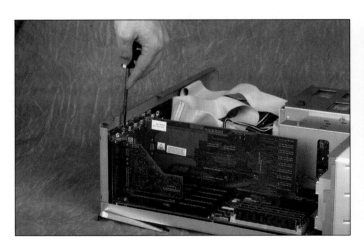

Fastening the retaining screw.

4 Once the card is fully seated in the adapter card slot, replace the retaining screw so it secures the adapter card in place.

Making internal cable connections.

5 Now make any necessary internal cable connections before you close up your PC. For instance, you may be installing a multi-function I/O card that has remote connectors that are connected to the I/O card via a ribbon cable. Make sure these ribbon cables are connected properly, according to the documentation that came with the I/O card.

CONFIGURING YOUR I/O CARD

Every device in your computer communicates with your PC through the use of interrupts. These IRQs (interrupt request lines) allow the device to demand attention from an otherwise busy CPU. The biggest task you need to perform when configuring your I/O card is to make sure that none of the IRQs conflict with other devices you have installed in your system.

How do you set IRQs? Typically through the use of jumpers on the adapter card, as specified by the card manufacturer.

Jumpers used to set configuration information for an I/O card.

These are used to configure the parallel port.

These are used to configure the serial ports.

Tip: *If you are upgrading all of your ports, and you are installing no more than two serial ports and one parallel port, then you probably can simply plug the card in and it will work fine. You should only change port configuration information if you know there will be an interrupt conflict causing a port (or ports) to quit working.*

One of the other things you may need to set for serial ports is the I/O address used by the serial port. This address only needs to be changed if you change the IRQ used for a particular port. These addresses also are set through the use of jumpers on the I/O card.

Why should you be concerned with these standard IRQ and I/O address settings? Primarily because they have become so standardized that software directed to use a specific serial port expects them to be used. It accesses the I/O addresses directly, and if you have changed them, you have a heck of a mess to clean up. (You know—misdirected data lying all over the place. Terribly hard to clean out of the carpet.)

Configuring cards for parallel ports is not nearly so complex. If you have only a single parallel port, simply leave it alone. If you have more than one, you will want to make sure the I/O address and IRQs are set properly.

STANDARD SERIAL I/O PORT ADDRESSES AND INTERRUPTS.

Serial Port	I/O Address	IRQ
COM1	3F8h	IRQ4
COM2	2F8h	IRQ3
COM3	3E8h	IRQ4
COM4	2E8h	IRQ3

STANDARD PARALLEL I/O PORT ADDRESSES AND INTERRUPTS.

Parallel Port	I/O Address	IRQ
LPT1	3BCh	IRQ7
LPT2	378h	IRQ5
LPT3	278h	None

As with the serial port configuration, you set parallel port information through the use of jumpers on the circuit board. Refer to the documentation provided with your I/O card for complete information on which jumpers to use.

After installing your ports, test them out. Connect your printers and other devices to the proper connectors. Boot your computer, and just sit back and observe. Did the mouse driver load? If not, then perhaps your serial port that the mouse is connected to is not configured properly. Next, try to print something. Did it print on the printer? If not, then you need to check the configuration of the parallel port.

If all else fails, you can use a software program such as MSD (the Microsoft Diagnostic Program, included with MS-DOS 6 and Windows) to figure out what is going on.

TROUBLESHOOTING PORT PROBLEMS

The most common problems with ports involve more than one device trying to use the same port. For example, your mouse and your modem may both be trying to use the same port, or interrupt setting (IRQ).

If you experience a problem immediately after adding a new port (or adding a new device to an existing port), chances are you have a port conflict problem. Try changing ports or IRQ settings for one of the external devices. This normally solves the problem.

Also, notice that conflicts can occur when devices hooked up to two nonconsecutive ports are used at the same time. In other words, if two devices are trying to use COM1 and COM3 (or COM2 and COM4) simultaneously, both could freeze up. This often happens when you have a mouse hooked up to COM1, and then hook a modem up to COM3. It all works fine until you try to use your mouse while your modem is working—then everything freezes up. The solution is simple: try not to use nonconsecutive ports in this manner.

If you have port problems, you're likely to encounter them with the following devices:

TROUBLESHOOTING MODEM PORTS

Problem: My software doesn't recognize the modem, or the modem won't dial.

- Confirm that all cables are connected properly and that the modem is on and connected to a phone line.

  Check which COM port the modem is attached to, and confirm that your software is set to use that COM port.

  If your modem is on COM1, make certain nothing else is using COM3. If your modem is connected to COM2, ensure that COM4 is not being used.

Problem: The modem dials, but all I get is random characters on-screen.

- Confirm that you are using the correct baud rate (speed) with your software. Set your baud rate at the highest speed your modem supports—it will adjust to slower modems if needed.

  Next, check that your communication setting matches those of the modem you are trying to call. Most systems use no parity, 8 data bits, and 1 stop bit—often referred to as "n,8,1". Set your software to these parameters and try again. If that doesn't work, try setting them to even parity, seven data bits, and one stop bit ("e,7,1").

TROUBLESHOOTING MOUSE PORTS

Problem: The mouse doesn't work at all.

- Check the cable connections to make certain the mouse cable is firmly seated in its port. Some mice, called "bus mice," have their own adapter card and use a round connector instead of the more common "D" shaped connector

  Make certain the mouse software is loaded. Mice rely on a software program called a "driver." The driver is the communication link between the mouse and the computer. Every mouse uses a driver—most are called MOUSE, or MSMOUSE. You need to run this program before your mouse will work.

  Check that the mouse isn't using a COM port that is sharing an interrupt line with another device (remember, COM1 and COM3 use the same interrupt, as do COM2 and COM4).

  If you already have two serial devices installed, a plotter and a mouse for example, you'll need to get a bus mouse and set its adapter card to an interrupt not already in use.

TROUBLESHOOTING PRINTER PORTS

Problem: Parallel printer doesn't print.

- Make certain all cables are connected properly and that the printer is on, loaded with paper, and the SELECT or ON LINE light is lit.

  Confirm that your software is using the parallel port.

  Check your AUTOEXEC.BAT file to confirm that the information is not being redirected to another port. If your AUTOEXEC.BAT has a line that looks like this:

  ```
  MODE COM1:=LPT1:
  ```

your printer output never gets to the parallel port; it is being rerouted to the serial port COM1!

Problem: Serial printer doesn't print.

- Check all the cables to make certain they are connected properly, that the printer is on and loaded with paper, and that the SELECT or ON LINE light is lit.

  Some printers require you to configure your serial port from either DOS or Windows. To configure your port, use the MODE command:

  ```
  MODE COM1:9600,n,8,1,p
  ```

  This sets COM1 to 9600 baud, no parity, 8 data bits, and 1 stop bit. The final "p" on the end prevents the printer from quiting when its buffer gets full by telling the computer to keep trying to send data until the printer catches up. Substitute COM2 above if your printer is attached to COM2.

  Configure your printer to match the settings of your COM port. You'll need to refer to your printer's manual for the settings and how to change them.

in

OVER

ODP4

SZ80

C303

INTE

CHAPTER 6
*Processors and
Coprocessors*

Understanding Processors

At the heart of your PC is a single chip, often called by different names. You may have heard it called a CPU (central processing unit), a microprocessor, or simply a processor. Processors come in all shapes, sizes, types, and capabilities. In the PC world, these processors are made by companies such as Intel, IBM, AMD, and Cyrix (but mostly Intel). There are several different types of CPUs made by Intel, each with different capabilities.

THE MAJOR CPU TYPES.

CPU	Comments
8086	Used in IBM PS/2 25 and 30 series computers
8088/8086	Used in the older IBM PCs,XTs and compatibles
80286	Used in the IBM PC/AT and compatible computers
80386	Used in second-generation AT-style systems
80486	Used in third-generation AT-style systems
Pentium	Just coming into wide use, also referred to as the 80586

Even though there are only five different base CPUs, you can have different types within each base CPU (such as the 80386SX or the 80486DX/2). These are variations on the main chip, with either subsets or supersets of performance and capabilities.

In general, determining which CPU you need is dictated by the type of software you want to run. If you want to run the latest Windows software, for example, you will need at least a system based on the 386 chip, preferably a fast 486SX chip. If you have more modest needs then you can definitely get by with the less-powerful CPUs. This need should be the basis of your decision. Once you have decided that you want to upgrade, there are a few other considerations you must take into account before you can make a decision about how to do that upgrade:

- **Clock speed.** Measured in megahertz (MHz), this is a fancy term that means nothing more than how fast the CPU can perform internal calculations. In general, the faster the clock speed, the more powerful the chip.

- **Bus Performance.** A bus is a pipeline from your CPU to other devices in your computer. The width and speed of this pipeline determines how fast (and how much) information can be moved to and from the CPU. It doesn't matter how fast your CPU is if your bus limits the amount and speed of data that can be processed.

- **Processor Expansion Options.** Some computers are designed to have their processors upgraded. These systems may have ZIF (zero insertion force) sockets that make replacing a processor much easier. Other systems may have an additional processor socket that allows you to install a new processor without removing the old one.

If your computer was manufactured in the past few years, there is a good chance you can easily upgrade the speed of your CPU. This is done by using what Intel calls an Overdrive chip, which is the same CPU with a faster clock speed. Thus, if your system has a 486 running at 33 MHz, you can get an Overdrive chip that will run at 66 MHz. This effectively doubles the speed at which your system operates.

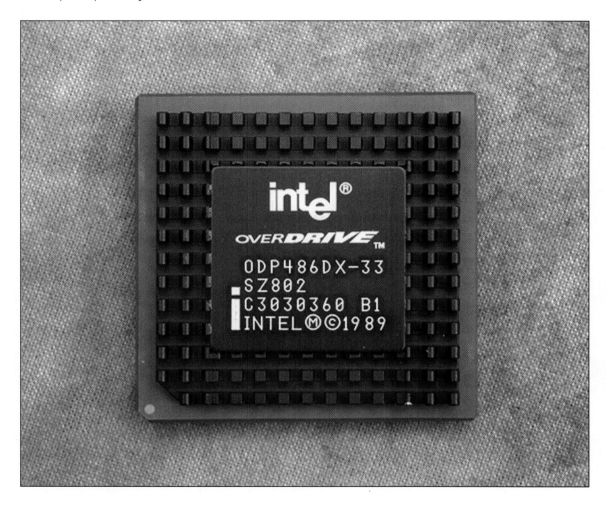

An Intel Overdrive chip, used to increase the speed at which your computer operates.

The Overdrive chips are identifiable by the Overdrive logo. Keep in mind that these chips use the faster speeds for internal operations. They still communicate with the "outside world" (all the other components in your system) at the slower non-multiplied speeds.

LOCATING THE PROCESSOR

Once you have removed the case from your system unit, start looking for the largest chip on the motherboard. On some newer systems, the chip will not even be soldered to the board; it will be in a plastic holder that makes it stand right out from the rest of the chips on the motherboard. This will be the CPU.

> **NOTE:** If you do locate the CPU and it is soldered into the motherboard, there is not much you can do to upgrade it.

The CPU. *The ZIF socket.*

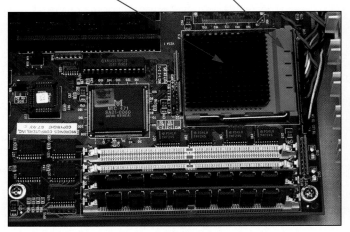

An example of the CPU in a system.

Some of the plastic holders on the newer systems use a ZIF socket. These allow you to easily remove and replace the CPU whenever necessary.

The CPU can be located in different places on different machines. The location depends on the size of your computer case and the orientation of the motherboard that holds the CPU. Generally, the smaller the case, the harder it is to get to the CPU. This doesn't mean it is impossible; it just means you have to dig a bit (so to speak) to get to where the CPU is located.

On the IBM PS/Valuepoint, for example, you must remove the computer cover and the disk drive housing assembly to get to the CPU. Don't despair! All you need to do is disconnect the drive cables, remembering how they were attached.

The mounting screws for the 3.5" disk drive.

There is another screw under here.

Remove this screw.

1 Once the cables are disconnected, take a look at the 3.5" disk drive. To remove this disk drive, you need to remove the two screws on each side of the drive (four screws total). Because of a rather awkward position for these screws, you may need a screwdriver with a rather long (4") blade.

The disk drive housing for the IBM PS/Valuepoint.

Remove this screw.

Remove these screws.

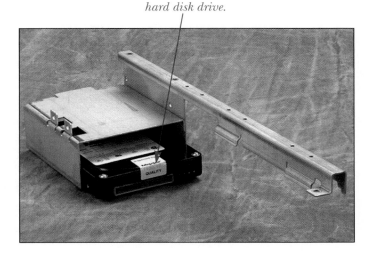

The rear of the hard disk drive.

The disk drive housing for the IBM PS/Valuepoint, removed from the computer system.

2 When these four screws are removed, slide the drive out of the front of the machine. Then, look at the disk drive housing itself. There are three screws to remove.

3 When these three screws are removed, the disk drive housing should lift right out.

A CPU with a heat sink attached.

Heat sinks attached to the top of the CPU.

Type of CPU.

Speed of CPU.

intel®
OVER**DRIVE**™
ODP486DX-33
SZ802
C3030360 B1
INTEL M©1989

Markings on a CPU.

Now that the disk drive housing is removed, look under where the disk drives were located. You should see the CPU sitting in its socket.

If you take a look at the processor—in any machine—you may see markings printed on the chip. The visibility of these markings depends on several things. First, how old the chip is (the markings may have worn off due to heating of the chip). They also may be hidden by additions made to the chip. Some chips have heat sinks attached that are used to help cool the CPU. This is particularly true of the newer chips, which run at high temperatures.

The heat sinks attached to some CPUs don't cover the entire chip. In these cases, there will be markings on the part of the chip without the heat sinks. These markings indicate the type of CPU you have installed in your system. Numbers such as 286 indicate an 80286, while 386 and 486, respectively, indicate an 80386 and 80486. At the end of the markings will be a dash and another number. This indicates the rated speed of the processor. For example, if a processor is labeled 80486-25, you have an 80486 processor rated for 25 MHz operation.

REMOVING THE PROCESSOR

If your system includes a ZIF socket for the CPU, removing it is a piece of cake. To do so, follow these steps:

1 Swing back the ZIF socket's lever.

2 Lift out the chip.

If your system does not have a ZIF socket, you need to be a little more careful in removing the CPU. Follow these steps:

1 Slip the edge of a small flat-blade screwdriver under the edge of the chip.

2 Rock the blade back and forth to slightly lift the edge of the CPU from the socket.

3 Insert the screwdriver blade under the opposite edge of the CPU and repeat the process.

4 Alternate the screwdriver blade between the two sides of the CPU, each time moving it a bit more out of the socket. By using this slow-but-steady technique, you will eventually get the CPU completely out of its socket and be able to lift it out with your fingers.

> **NOTE:** If you use the screwdriver method of chip removal, be careful that you don't force the chip to an angle that is too oblique. Doing so could bend the pins remaining within the socket.

REPLACING THE PROCESSOR

Now that the CPU is out of the socket, take a look at the socket itself. Notice that there is one corner of the socket that is notched or beveled. This is the "pin 1" position, and is extremely important. Regardless of the type of socket your system uses, this same technique of marking the socket is used.

Notice the notched corner.   *The pin 1 position also is marked.*

An empty ZIF socket for a CPU.

Notice the notched corner.

An Intel Overdrive CPU.

If you look at the replacement CPU (in this case, an Overdrive chip), you will see that it, too, has a notch.

These notched corners—the one on the CPU and the one on the socket—must line up. If you don't line them up the CPU will not insert properly in the socket, and you won't be able to use your system.

Once you have located the notched corners on the processor and socket, follow these steps to install the new processor:

Notice the notched corners line up.

Lever is completely closed.

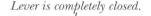

1 Place the CPU in the socket, making sure the notches line up. If your system has a ZIF socket, you should not have to force the CPU into the socket; it should drop in freely.

2 If you have the ZIF socket, the final step is to swing the lever back to its closed position. If you do not have the ZIF type of socket, make sure the pins align properly, and then gently push the CPU straight down into the socket.

UNDERSTANDING COPROCESSORS

Until the introduction of the 80486, the CPU had a companion chip, called the NPU (numeric processor unit) that helped speed up numeric operations within the computer. This chip used the same numbering system as the CPUs, except it ended in a seven. Thus, the proper NPU to use with the 80286 is the 80287, and the proper one to use with the 80386 is the 80387.

Do you need a numeric coprocessor? Yes and no. If you have a system that uses an 80486 DX or Pentium processor, then you do not need an NPU; numeric operations are built into the main CPU. If you don't use math-intensive software, then you won't benefit by having an NPU.

However, if you do use math-intensive software (such as CAD software or heavy-duty spreadsheets), then you might benefit from a coprocessor. The best way to discover if you would benefit from the use of an NPU is to examine the documentation that comes with your software. If it can take advantage of an NPU, and you use the software quite a bit, then you will benefit if you install one.

Assuming you decide to install an NPU, you must next be concerned with getting the right one. Like your CPU, the NPU is rated for different operational speeds. To get the right NPU, you must match the speed of the NPU with the speed of your CPU. Thus, if you have a 25 MHz 80386, then you will need a 25 MHz 80387.

> **NOTE:** You can use an NPU that is rated at a speed faster than your CPU; this won't hurt your system a bit. However, if you use an NPU rated for a slower speed than your CPU, you will not realize any speed improvements by adding the chip. In addition, you could experience intermittent software problems or complete chip failure because you are trying to run the NPU at a speed faster than the speed for which it was designed.

ADDING THE COPROCESSOR

Adding a coprocessor is an easy task. Most systems that can accept an NPU are designed with an empty socket next to the CPU. Take a look inside your system. If you locate the CPU, you should see such a socket next to it.

This is the socket for the NPU. *This signifies the pin 1 position.* *This is the CPU.*

The notch (and the dot) indicates the pin 1 position.

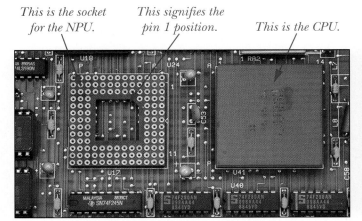

The CPU and empty NPU socket. *An Intel 80387 NPU chip.*

As with the CPUs mentioned earlier, notice that the NPU socket has a notch that indicates where pin 1 is located. In this instance, the notch is on the inside of the socket (but it still indicates the correct corner for pin 1).

Once you have located the notched corners on the processor and socket, follow these steps to install the new processor:

Tip: *Once the coprocessor is installed, make sure you change any configuration information in your software that is necessary for it to take advantage of the NPU chip.*

① Align the pin 1 indicators and place the chip in the socket.

② If all pins are aligned, you can press down on the chip to insert it fully into the socket.

CHAPTER 7
System Memory

UNDERSTANDING MEMORY

System memory, usually referred to as RAM (Random Access Memory), is a high-speed work area. Your computer moves information and any associated data into RAM before it begins working with them. RAM is only temporary storage. When the power is turned off, the information stored in RAM is lost—which is why it is important that you save your data to a floppy or hard disk drive before you turn off your computer or exit a program. This chapter shows you how to identify different types of memory and how to add additional RAM to your computer.

You can purchase high-quality random-access memory chips from any of a number of sources and install them yourself. By following the directions in this chapter you can be up and running in no time, particularly if your system uses SIMMs (single in-line memory modules).

How memory is packaged has changed over the years. When the PC was first introduced (indeed, up to about two years ago), memory typically came packaged in individual chips.

Common examples of memory chips.

Memory chip pins.

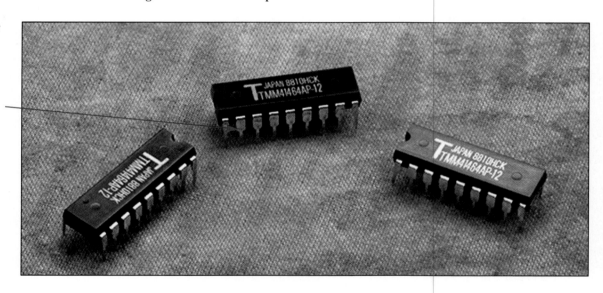

These chips are technically referred to as DIPPs (dual in-line pin packages). Nine of these chips, inserted in a row in your system, represent a single bank of memory. Each chip bank represents a specific quantity of memory—256K.

The problem in working with memory chips is that they aren't easy to install. Not impossible; just a pain. It is relatively easy to bend and possibly break any one of the chip's 18 metal pins or not get them inserted properly.

In more recent times, memory has been packaged in SIMMs. This module consists of an entire bank of memory. Basically, the individual memory chips are smaller now and are mounted on the module board. (There are still nine memory chips making up the entire bank of memory; the ninth chip is on the back of the SIMM.) As you might imagine from looking at them, SIMMs are much easier to work with than the individual memory chips.

An example of a memory SIMM.

Once you have determined the physical characteristics of the memory used by your system, there are two primary specifications of which you need to be aware:

- **Memory Capacity.** One of the primary specifications of memory is its size. This does not refer to the physical size of the memory chips or the SIMMs, but to the data capacity of the memory. In the early days of the PC, 16K memory chips were commonly available. Later, memory size increased; in today's systems, it is not uncommon to use 1M, 4M, or 16M memory chips.

- **Memory Speed.** RAM is available in a variety of speeds, measured in nanoseconds (ns), where a nanosecond is one billionth of a second. In PC systems, memory speeds typically range anywhere from 20ns to 200ns, with chips in the 50ns to 120ns range being the most common.

Tip: Regardless of the type of system you have, you should never mix memory chips or SIMMs of different sizes. This means that all of the chips or all of the SIMMs in your system should be the same size.

MEMORY MANAGEMENT

Entire books can be (and have been) written about how to best use memory. This entire area of study is called memory management. It also is the purpose of some special systems software, referred to as memory managers.

This does not mean, however, that you should avoid the topic. On the contrary, effective and efficient use of the memory within your system is a worthy goal for every PC user.

If you have MS-DOS 6.0 or 6.2, memory management is as easy as invoking a DOS command. When you use the **MEMMAKER** command (from the DOS prompt), DOS will analyze the memory on your system and automatically configure it for the best possible performance.

CHOOSING THE RIGHT MEMORY

Tip: *Remember that software packages pro-*
vide only minimum requirements. Sometimes
you also will see information on the recom-
mended memory configuration. In these cases,
use the recommended configuration in prefer-
ence to the minimum.

The right amount of memory for your system is a mixture of what your soft-ware requires and what you personally desire. If you take a look at your soft-ware packages, you will find that somewhere on the box (or in the first chap-ter of the installation manual) you will find information about the minimum memory requirements. If you take a look at all of the software you use, you can select the largest memory requirement out of all the packages, and then use that as the beginning point.

Once you know your starting point, your personal preference can kick in. Your most memory-hungry software may require a minimum of 4M. There is a good chance you will want to double this, however, so that you can get bet-ter overall performance. Typically, the more memory you have to spare, the better off you will be.

> **NOTE:** It is rare, but some hardware or software devices have an upper memory limit. The one that comes to mind first is the Video Blaster by Creative Labs. With this hardware board and its associated software, you must have less than 16M installed in your system. The only solution is to either accept the memory limitation or find a different video board.

Once you have determined the amount of memory you need (or would like), you must determine if your system will handle that much. You may already know that different CPUs allow you to access different amounts of memory. An 80486, for example, can address up to 4 gigabytes (a gigabyte is equal to 1000 megabytes) of memory. Remember, however, that there is a difference between what can be addressed and what is available. The design of your motherboard is the limiting factor in adding memory to your system.

Most motherboards available today allow you a maximum of either 16M, 32M, or 64M of memory. And many of the systems have a limited number of SIMM connectors (typically either four or eight). Thus, to fit 64M in only four SIMM connectors, you would use 16M SIMMs. To make sure what your system will handle, refer to your system documentation or call your computer distributor. Unfortunately, if your system will not handle the amount of memory you need, your only option may be to get a different motherboard.

LOCATING YOUR MEMORY

Once you open your computer case, the memory area is typically easy to spot. If your system uses memory chips, the memory area appears as the most symmetrical area of chips on your motherboard.

Rows of memory chips on a motherboard.

If your system uses SIMMs, the memory is just as easy to locate.

SIMMs installed on a motherboard.

Installed SIMM.

Empty SIMM slots.

REMOVING MEMORY CHIPS

If you are replacing memory, you need to know how to remove it. If you have the older memory chips, you remove them as you do almost any type of chip. While you can use a special chip puller, it is easier to at least start by using a small flat-blade screwdriver, as described in the following steps:

1 Insert the screwdriver blade under the edge of the chip you want to remove.

2 Pry the chip upward until it is in approximately the position shown in the picture.

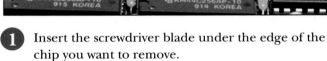

3 Slide the screwdriver blade under the opposite edge of the chip and pry it upward.

4 Now you can use the chip puller to easily extract the memory chip. You will need to repeat the process for each memory chip you want removed.

REMOVING SIMMS

Removing SIMMs is easier than removing memory chips. You don't need any tools; the SIMMS are large enough to be easily handled and they are not as fragile as memory chips. Read through these steps to learn how to remove a SIMM:

1 Take a look at how the SIMM is held in place. Each end of the SIMM is held in place by a small clip.

Looking closely at one end of a SIMM.

Pull this back to release the SIMM.

2 Unclip each end of the SIMM, and it springs forward a bit.

3 You now can remove the SIMM from its slot easily.

INSTALLING MEMORY CHIPS

Installing memory chips isn't difficult. You just align the notch on the memory chip with the notch in the socket, get each of the memory chip's pins carefully started in the socket's holes, and press the chip in firmly. To do so, follow these steps:

Alignment notch on socket.

Make sure there is no dust or debris in the holes.

Alignment notch on chip.

This alignment notch should align with the one in the socket.

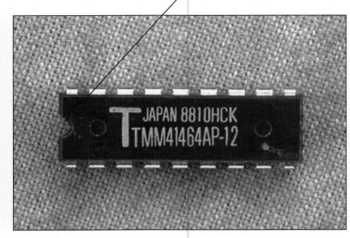

1 If your system uses memory chips, you should examine the socket into which you will be placing the memory chip.

2 Now take a look at the memory chip itself. You will need to make sure the chip aligns properly with the socket. This is done by matching up the alignment notch in the socket and the chip.

3 Place the chip on the socket and apply smooth, even pressure to firmly seat the chip. As you are inserting the chip, make sure that all the pins are going into the holes. If they do not, the chip will not work properly.

NOTE: You may need to bend the memory chip pins inward just a little in order for the pins to line up with the holes in the socket. If you do so, make sure you bend all the pins the same amount. Remember that the pins are fragile, and bending them too much can break them. (If you break a pin on a memory chip, it is useless. You will need to replace the chip.)

USING A SPECIAL TOOL

Rather than inserting memory chips by hand, you can use a special chip insertion tool. This tool is included in many toolkits you can purchase. The chip rests inside the end of the tool, helping to keep the pins straight and at the proper angle. When you use the tool, you push down on a plunger mechanism that applies even pressure to the entire chip, thereby seating it evenly in the socket.

INSERTING SIMM MODULES

If your system uses SIMMs, count yourself lucky. They are much easier to insert than are the older memory chips. There also is less chance of messing up the chips, since there are no pins to bend or break. The following steps show you how to upgrade SIMM memory.

Notice the angle at which the SIMM is being inserted.

This alignment notch should align with the one in the socket.

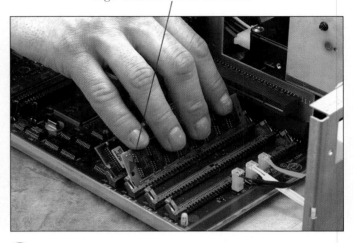

1 Hold the SIMM by the top edge and insert it at an angle in the SIMM slot.

2 Applying even pressure across the entire SIMM, rock it backwards until it locks into place.

NOTE: Always fill SIMM slots in order, beginning with the lowest number. The number of the SIMM slot is typically printed on the motherboard.

Make sure the SIMM is locked in place.

3 When the SIMM is locked fully in place, it will appear as shown.

MAKING YOUR SYSTEM WORK

Depending on the type of BIOS you have installed in your system, your memory addition may work right off the bat. If it doesn't, you will receive an error when you first boot your system. In this case, you will need to access your CMOS setup routines to change your memory settings. These settings must reflect the entire amount of memory installed in your system; otherwise the computer thinks there may be an error. After you have changed the settings, save them and reboot your computer.

In rare cases (particularly with older PCs), you may have to adjust jumpers or switch settings on your motherboard. If you suspect this is the case, refer to your system documentation or contact your computer supplier.

CAUTION: Never force a SIMM in or out of its slot. Doing so will not necessarily damage the SIMM, but will damage the slot that holds it. If this damage is inflicted, you may not be able to secure the memory in place. This will make the SIMM unusable and you will need to purchase a new motherboard.

CHAPTER 8
Floppy Disk Drives

UNDERSTANDING FLOPPY DISK DRIVES

As any seasoned PC user knows, floppy disks come in a variety of shapes, sizes, and capacities. Each of these floppy disks is used in different types of drives. There are two predominant sizes of floppy disks in the PC world— 5.25" and 3.5" disks. This is only the physical size of the disk, however. Each size has different data capacities. For instance, 5.25" disks can either store 360K or 1.2M of data. The 3.5" disks can store either 720K, 1.44M, or 2.88M of data.

Not all disk drives can read and write to each of the different capacity disks. For instance, if you have a 360K 5.25" disk drive, you can read and write to only those disks—you cannot access the high density (1.2M) 5.25" disks. However, if you have a disk drive that can read or write to the higher capacities, it will also read and write to the lower capacities.

There are many different physical appearances for floppy drives. Today nearly all drives are configured in what is called a "half-height" format. This simply means that the drive casing is approximately 1.75" high. In the early days of PCs, full-height drives were twice this high; it was considered a big step forward when the smaller profile drives made their debut.

The 3.5" disk drives are typically a little smaller; only about 1" in height. These drives usually fit in a holder that occupies the same height as the other drives (1.75") or into a special receptacle in the computer case that is specially made for the smaller drive size.

A common 5.25"
disk drive.

Half-height drives
are approximately
1.75" in height.

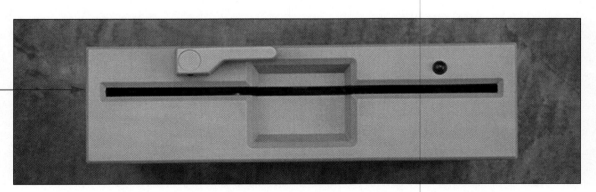

A common 3.5"
disk drive.

Approximately
1" high, without
a holder.

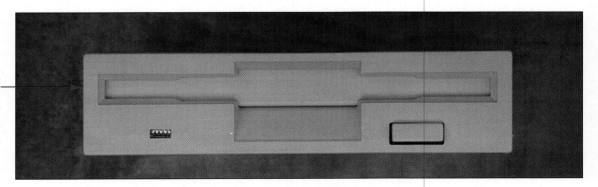

Lately, there has been another exciting development in floppy drives. Some vendors have started marketing a combined 5.25" and 3.5" drive that both fit in a single half-height space (1.75").

A combination 3.5" and 5.25" disk drive.

3.5" disk drive.

5.25" disk drive.

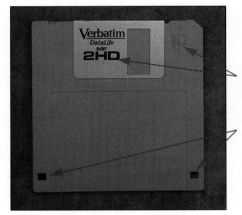

A 1.44M 3.5" disk.

Indicates this is a high-density disk.

This capacity disk has two holes.

A 1.2M 5.25" disk.

This capacity disk has no hub ring.

TELLING FLOPPY DISKS APART

How can you determine the capacity of floppy disks? You can't always rely on a label. After all, it may be missing or covered up. Determining the capacity is quite easy, provided you remember a few simple rules.

- 2.88M 3.5" disks have ED (extra density) stamped in the corner of the shell.

- 1.44M 3.5" disks always have two holes in the shell. Generally, they also have HD (high density) stamped in the corner of the shell.

- 720K 3.5" disks have only one hole in the shell.

- 1.2M 5.25" disks do not have a hub ring in the center of the disk.

- 360K 5.25" disks have a hub ring in the center of the disk.

REMOVING A FLOPPY DRIVE

Once your computer case is removed, locate the drive you want to remove and then look at the back of the drive. Whether the drive is a 5.25" or 3.5" drive, the cable connections are effectively the same. There are two cables; one is for power and the other for data.

Removing the data cable.

1 Remove the data cable; this is a flat ribbon cable that you can remove from the back of the drive. Feel free to pull on the cable itself. Fold the cable back out of the way so that you can continue to work on the drive.

Removing the power cable.

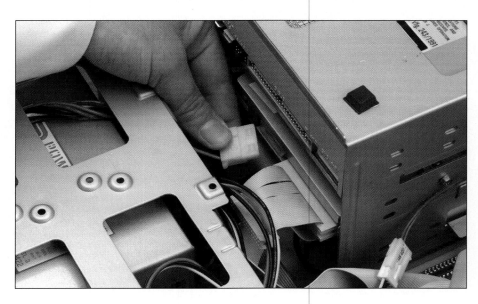

Tip: *You may have noticed that the power plugs for the 3.5" and 5.25" drives are different. The one for the 3.5" drive is a bit smaller and there may be a small clip holding the plug into the socket. Make sure you disengage this clip before removing the plug.*

2 Remove the power cable; this is the one that has the four individual colored wires going into a white plug. Removing this cable can be troublesome; it tends to be very tight. Make sure you remove this cable by pulling on the plug, not on the wires themselves. You may need to wiggle the plug back and forth in order to get it out. Once it is removed, fold it back as well, remembering where you put it.

Typical disk drive mounting screws.

Remove this screw.

There is another screw under here and more on the other side.

3 Now that the cables are removed, you can unfasten the drive itself. This is done by first examining the mounting brackets to which the drive is attached. There are screws on the left and right sides of the drive that attach the drive to the computer case.

NOTE: Depending on how the computer system was originally assembled, there may be either one or two screws on each side of the disk drive.

Sliding the drive out of the front of the PC.

4 When these screws are removed, you can slide the drive out of the front of the machine.

ADDING A FLOPPY DRIVE

Adding a floppy drive is almost exactly the opposite process of removing one. Once you have removed the computer case, it is a relatively easy task. Perhaps the hardest part is deciding which drive bay you want to use for the disk drive.

Tip: *Make sure you select a bay that your power cable and data cable will reach.*

Different computer cases have different configurations of drive bays. Some have quite a few, others have only one or two. Some even have special bays for particular disk drives (for instance, a smaller bay for 3.5" drives). You need to decide in which bay you want the floppy drive located.

If your power and data cables are long enough, you can attach them before you slide the drive into the case.

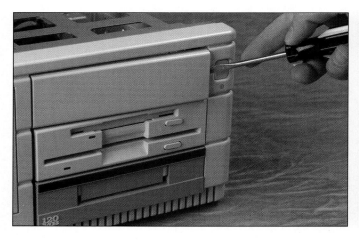

Removing the plastic panel from the front of a PC.

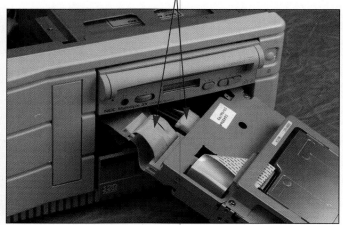

Inserting a disk into the drive bay.

1 Once you decide on a bay, you may need to remove a plastic panel from the front of the computer case. This panel is used to cover the part of the bay that will be occupied by your new drive. The panel may either be a part of the computer case itself, or part of the cover that attaches to the case. Simply use a small screwdriver to pop the panel out.

2 Slide the disk drive through the front of the computer case into the bay. (If the disk drive does not fill the full width of the drive bay, refer to the sidebar.) Don't screw the drive in place yet; it is easier to connect the cables to the rear of the drive if you can still slide it back and forth.

MAKING YOUR DRIVE WIDER

Some of the newer disk drives are smaller than the bays designed to hold them. This is because the drive bays have been designed for the widest standard drive—the 5.25" disk drive. To secure the smaller 3.5" disk drives in this bay, you need a drive adapter kit, available from wherever you purchase your disk drives.

One of the adapters attaches to each side of the disk drive, and then the adapters, in turn, attach to the computer case.

Drive adapters used to secure a 3.5" drive in a 5.25" drive bay.

Power cable and plug for a 5.25" disk drive.

Power cable and plug for a 3.5" disk drive.

3 Connect the cables to the rear of the drive. There are only two cables to connect—one for the power and the other for the controller. The power cable is the one that has the four individual colored wires running into a white plug. Because of the way that the power plug is molded, there is only one way to plug it in.

Looking at the back of a disk drive.

This is for the power cable.

This is for the controller cable.

4 Once the power plug is connected, you can connect the controller cable. This is the cable that runs from the disk drive controller to the floppy drives. Take a look at the cable and notice that there is more than one plug on the cable, and not all the plugs are of the same type. You should match the plug with the connector on the back of your disk drive. If you follow the cable from the disk controller toward the disk drives, the first drive you come to is the A: drive, and the second is the B: drive. Thus, you can completely control which drive your system considers A: and B:.

NOTE: If you swap your A: and B: drive, you need to change your CMOS settings to reflect what type of drives are connected to the A: and B: positions. If you do not, your system will not work properly.

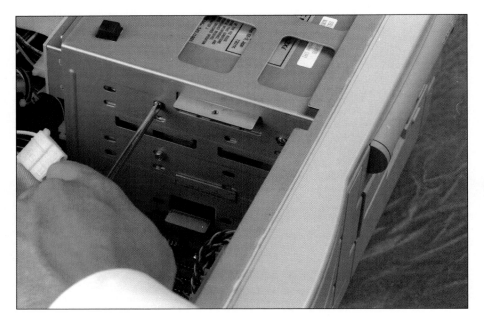

Tightening the screws on a disk drive.

5 Now that you are through connecting cables, you can tighten the screws that hold your disk drive in place. Slide it in or out until it is positioned correctly for your computer case. Then tighten the screws on both sides of the drive.

TROUBLESHOOTING FLOPPY DISK DRIVE PROBLEMS

Most problems with floppy disk drives are really problems with floppy disks. About the only real drive problems you may encounter are incorrect connections (hooking drive A: up to cable B:, for example), bad connections, and plain old bad drives. Pretty much everything else is either user error or a bad disk.

Problem: There's an error on-screen that says "Nonsystem disk or disk error." I'm just trying to boot up; what could be the problem?

- Typically, this is caused by a blank disk or a data disk being in the A: drive when you are trying to boot your system. Remove any disk and try again.

  If you get the error when you are sure that you are booting to the C: drive, then the error is much more serious. This means that something has happened to damage the boot record or some other vital information on your hard disk. Turn your machine off and seek the help of the most technical person you know.

Problem: I have this floppy disk full of neat games from my friend. Why can't I read it in my floppy drive?

- Different floppy disks have different capacities. It is possible that your friend used a disk that is a higher capacity than what you can read on your system. Check this out first.

  Different types of computers format their disks in different ways. Check to see if the disk is originally from a Macintosh or Amiga system.

  If you are sure you can read the same capacity as your friend does, and the disk is not from another type of system, then it may mean that either your friend's disk drive or your's is out of alignment and is in need of service. Only a qualified disk technician can answer which machine needs service.

Problem: I tried to read from (or write to) my floppy disk drive, and my system wouldn't let me do it. What's wrong?

- First, check to make sure you really have a disk in the drive—and that the disk is fully inserted and (if it's a 5.25" disk) the drive door is closed.

  Next, check to see if the disk is formatted; your system can't read or write nonformatted disks.

  Finally, check to make sure you actually typed the right drive letter. (This little mistake causes a lot of so-called problems.)

Problem: I tried to format a disk and received a DOS error message that said "Attempted write-protect violation." What's up?

- You're trying to format a floppy disk that is write-protected. Remove the write-protect tab (on 5.25" disks) or move the write-protect shutter to close the hole (on 3.5" disks). Then restart the operation.

Problem: I tried to format a disk and received a DOS error message that said "Invalid media or Track 0 bad--disk unusable" (or "Write failure, disk unusable"). What did I do wrong?

- You have probably tried to format a low density floppy disk in a high density drive. Try reformatting the disk at a lower density. If that doesn't work, the disk is damaged. Throw it away and start again with a new one.

Problem: I am not certain which one of my floppy drives is drive A:

- There are two things you may want to identify about your floppy drives—which drive is drive A:, and what the capacity of that drive is. Unfortunately, you can't always rely on the physical location of a disk drive within your computer case to indicate which drive is A: and which is B:.

Is drive A: on top or on bottom in this picture?

One of the easiest ways to get this information is to actually stick a disk in the drive, and then try to pull up a directory for that drive. Do that by typing:

```
dir a:
```

If the drive is accessed, it is drive A:. If not, it is drive B:. You should then mark your drives so you (and others) know which drive is which.

Problem: I don't know if my floppy drive is a high- or low-capacity drive.

- If you want to discover the capacity of your disk drive, simply put a blank disk in the drive and try to format it, as in the following:

```
format a: /u
```

The FORMAT command always tries to format at the largest appropriate capacity for the disk drive. Thus, if it is a 1.44M 3.5" disk drive, it tries to format the disk as 1.44M. When FORMAT tells you how it is formatting the disk, you will then discover the disk drive's capacity.

CHAPTER 9
Hard Disk Drives

UNDERSTANDING HARD DISK DRIVES

Hard disk drives store large amounts of data on your computer system. Hard disk drives range in capacity from 20M to 400M—and more. Hard disks consist of numerous metallic platters that store data magnetically. Special read/write heads realign the magnetic particles on the platters, much like recording head records data onto magnetic recording tape.

Hard disk drives are almost a commodity item these days. All you need to do is decide on the specifications you want in your drive, and then pick the vendor with the lowest cost. While a complete discussion of hard drive specifications is beyond the scope of this book, you may want to pay attention to the following items when considering a new hard disk drive:

- **Type of Drive.** If you are adding the hard drive to your current system, is it the same type you are already using? It must be if you are going to use the same controller. If you are replacing your current drive, you may need to purchase a new controller as well.

- **Capacity.** How much data does the disk drive hold? In today's market, it is not advisable to purchase a disk drive that has less than 200M.

- **Speed.** This refers to how fast you can access data on the drive. Times are always measured in microseconds; fast drives have access times around eight microseconds. Get the fastest drive you can, because this is the biggest contributing factor to overall system performance.

- **Seek Time.** This refers to how fast the disk drive mechanism can find data on a different track. As a rule, faster is better.

- **Buffer.** If the disk drive has a cache buffer, it can provide faster apparent throughput of your data by storing frequently accessed data in high-speed memory.

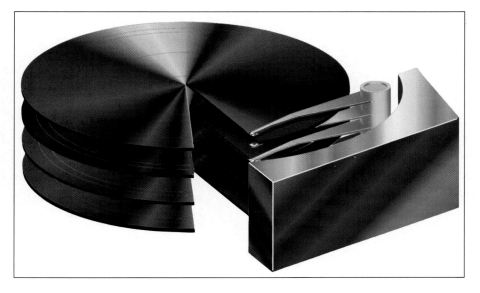

Of course, there are other things to consider about the hard drive. For example, you may be interested to know the physical size of the drive (3.5" is standard today, but you also can find some that are 5.25") and whether it is internal or external.

The inside of a hard disk drive.

UNDERSTANDING CONTROLLERS

Drive controllers are responsible for the successful operation of any number of attached drives. It is not unusual to have a disk drive controller that can run two floppy drives and two or three hard drives. You can even attach a tape drive or a CD-ROM to the controller; they all operate through the same basic rules.

There are many types of controllers available; the one you use is largely a function of the type of hard drive you have installed in your system. If you have an IDE drive, for example, you have an IDE controller.

> **NOTE:** Many controllers are able to interface with more than one type of device. For example, SCSI devices obviously require SCSI compatible controllers. Some SCSI controllers, however, may include separate connectors for non-SCSI devices such as floppy drives or external speakers.

There are typically four types of hard disk controllers available today:

- **ST-506/412**. Developed around 1980 by Seagate Technologies, this is the oldest technology, and the one that is in the most number of older systems. It also has the worst performance characteristics of any of the disk controllers; this controller is not widely used in new systems.

- **ESDI**. This stands for Enhanced Small Device Interface. Led by Maxtor, a group of drive manufacturers came up with this controller interface in 1983. It featured higher performance and greater reliability than the earlier standard. ESDI controllers became quite prevalent in high-end systems in the mid-to-late 1980s. They are not recommended for systems today, however, because they are not quite as fast or reliable as the newer controllers.

- **IDE**. Today the majority of hard disk drives use IDE controllers. IDE stands for Integrated Drive Electronics, meaning that the actual controller is built into the hard drive. This type of design allows for greater reliability and ease of installation. However, because the controller electronics are in the hard disk, there are possible compatibility problems if you want to install IDE drives from different companies into the same system.

- **SCSI**. This stands for Small Computer Systems Interface. Technically, this is not a type of disk controller, but a bus definition. It can be used for connecting up to eight different devices (not just hard drives). Hard drives that work with SCSI interfaces have traditionally been high capacity, high performance drives, and that has led to the interface being used in high-end systems. Many other types of systems are now using them, because a single card can control a large number of different devices on your system.

REMOVING A HARD DISK DRIVE

Removing a hard drive from your system is very similar to removing a floppy drive.

> **NOTE:** Depending on how your system case has been assembled, you may need to remove the floppy disk drives before you can get to the hard disk. If you need to, read the earlier section about removing a floppy disk drive.

1 Take the case off your system, and locate the drive you want to remove. Look at the back of the hard disk drive, and you will see that (as with the floppy drives) there are two cables. One is for power, and the other for data.

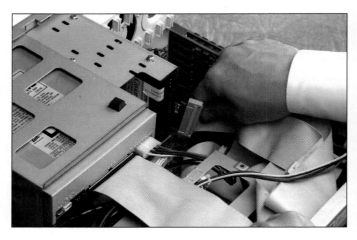

Removing the data cable.

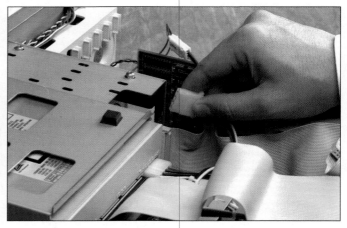

Removing the power cable.

2 Remove the data cable. This is the flat ribbon cable, and is the easiest to remove. Feel free to pull on the cable itself; it is strong enough. Once the cable is disconnected, fold it out of the way so you can continue to work on the drive.

3 Remove the power cable; this is the one that has the four individual colored wires going into a white plug. As with any drive power cable, removing it can be troublesome—not because it is hard to get at, but because it is always quite tight. Make sure you remove this cable by pulling on the plug, not on the wires. You may need to wiggle the plug back and forth in order to get it out. Once it is removed, fold it back out of the way.

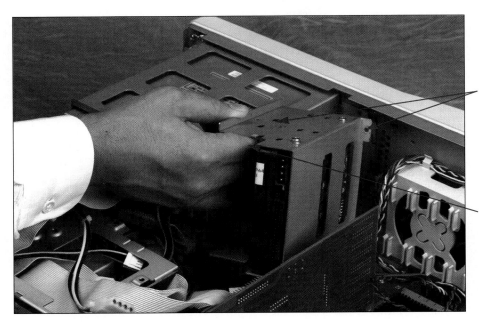

Removing the drive bay.

This drive bay was held in by two screws.

Once the screws have been removed, carefully remove the drive bay.

4 Many new computers have separate drive bays for internal hard drives. In most cases you will need to remove the entire drive bay before you can remove the hard drive.

Removing the screws.

5 Remove the screws that hold the drive to the drive bay. Look at both the left and right sides of the drive and you should see one or two retaining screws on each side.

The hard disk free from the drive bay.

6 Take the drive out of the drive bay.

NOTE: Remember that when you remove the hard disk drive, you cannot boot your system to the hard drive any more. Make sure you have a bootable disk handy in case you need to reboot your system.

ADDING A HARD DISK DRIVE

Adding a hard disk drive is similar to adding any other type of disk drive. Some hard disk drives are mounted in internal drive bays that are specifically designed to hold disk drives. The following steps show you how to add a hard drive to your computer:

1 Remove the computer case, and decide which drive bay you want to use.

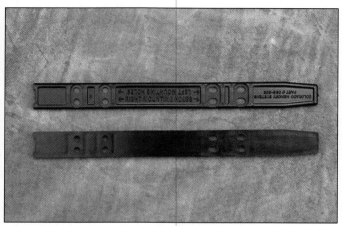

Adapter kits allow 3.5" disk drives to fit into larger 5.25" drive bays.

Drive rails are used primarily in older PCs, XTs, ATs, and compatibles.

2 Check to see if your hard drive fits the available slot. You may need to purchase an adapter kit to widen the drive, or drive rails that slide into the drive bay.

Hard drive installed in drive bay.

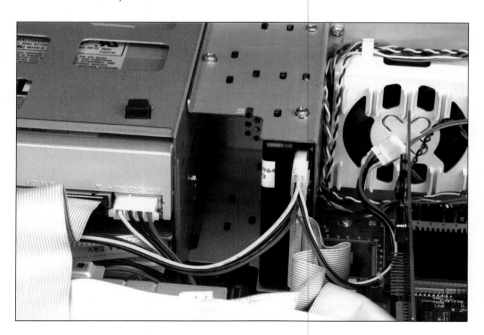

3 Fasten the disk drive into the drive bay you want to use; make sure the back of the disk drive is pointed toward the rear of the drive bay, and then replace the entire drive bay in the computer.

> **NOTE:** If you are installing a computer in a standard drive bay—like those where your floppy drive is located—slide the drive into the drive bay gently, attach the power and data cables, and then screw the drive in place.

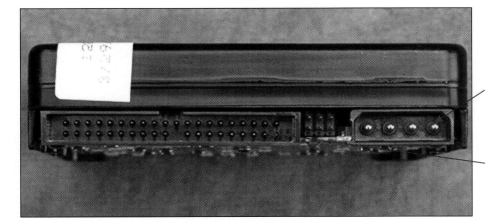

Looking at the back of a hard disk drive.

This is for the power plug.

This is for the controller cable.

4 Connect the power cable to the disk drive; this is the cable that has the four individual colored wires running into a white plug (it is the same type of plug discussed earlier with 5.25" floppy drives). Because of the way the power plug is molded, there is only one correct way to plug it in.

5 Once the power cable is connected, connect the controller cable; this is the cable that runs from the disk drive controller to the hard drives. If you are installing a brand new disk controller, you need to remove the old one first. You do not need to insert the new controller card yet, because it is easier to connect cables to it while it is not installed in a slot.

> **NOTE:** You can connect more than one hard disk drive to the same disk controller; that is why there are more than two plugs on the cable. It is possible that if you have more than one hard disk connected to your disk controller, you need to adjust jumper switches either on the controller, on the drive, or both. Check the documentation for your controller card to discover the answer.

TROUBLESHOOTING HARD DISK DRIVE PROBLEMS

Hard disk drive problems are among the most common problems for computer users. Because the disk platters are almost constantly in motion, many problems are caused by general wear and tear. Many minor surface problems can be fixed (or masked) by using a general-purpose utility program like Norton Disk Doctor. Once a hard disk drive deteriorates too far, however, it's better to replace it than risk further data loss.

PROBLEM: I just received a DOS error message that said "Cannot read file allocation table, File allocation table bad, drive C:." What happened?

- This is not good. Your FAT (File Allocation Table) is unreadable. First, try to repair the damage with a commercial disk utility like those found in Symantec's Norton Utilities. If you have DOS 6.2, you can try using SCAN-DISK.

  If these utilities don't help, you may need to reformat the disk drive. In cases where the drive can't reliably store data, you should replace the drive.

PROBLEM: DOS just gave me an error message that said "Sector not found." What does this mean?

- This generally means your hard disk is developing a bad spot. Again, try to repair the damage with a commercial disk utility like those found in Symantec's Norton Utilities. If you have DOS 6.2, you can try using SCAN-DISK.

PROBLEM: I just saw an error on-screen that says "Nonsystem disk or disk error." I'm just trying to boot up. What could be the problem?

- Typically this is caused by a blank disk or a data disk being in the A: drive when you are trying to boot your system. Remove any disk and try again.

  If you get the error when you are sure that you are booting to the C: drive, the error is much more serious. This means that something has happened to damage the boot record or some other vital information on your hard disk.

  If you created an emergency boot disk as shown in Chapter 2, "Before You Upgrade: Taking Precautions," you are in luck. Insert the disk in the disk drive and re-boot your computer. Then, from the A: prompt, type SYS C: to make your drive bootable again.

  If you don't have an emergency boot disk, boot your system with your original DOS disk and then use the SYS command to make your hard drive bootable.

PROBLEM: My disk is running slower than usual. How can I speed it up?

- This problem is most often caused when the data on your disk has become fragmented. If you're running DOS 6, you can run the Defragmenter utility by typing the following at the DOS prompt:

  `DEFRAG`

  If you're running an older version of DOS, you can obtain the same results by running a third-party defragmenter utility, such as Norton Speed Disk.

PROBLEM: I accidentally formatted my hard disk. What do I do now?

- If you have DOS 5 or 6, you can use the DOS UNFORMAT utility to undo that accidental format. If you're using DOS 6 and using its mirror utility, type the following at the DOS prompt:

  `UNFORMAT C:`

  If you're using an older version of DOS, you're out of luck. (Although if you have recently backed up your data, you can restore it to your newly-formatted hard disk.)

  NOTE: The UNFORMAT command works much better if you use the MIRROR utility. The MIRROR utility keeps track of vital hard drive information that makes it much easier to UNFORMAT a disk drive.

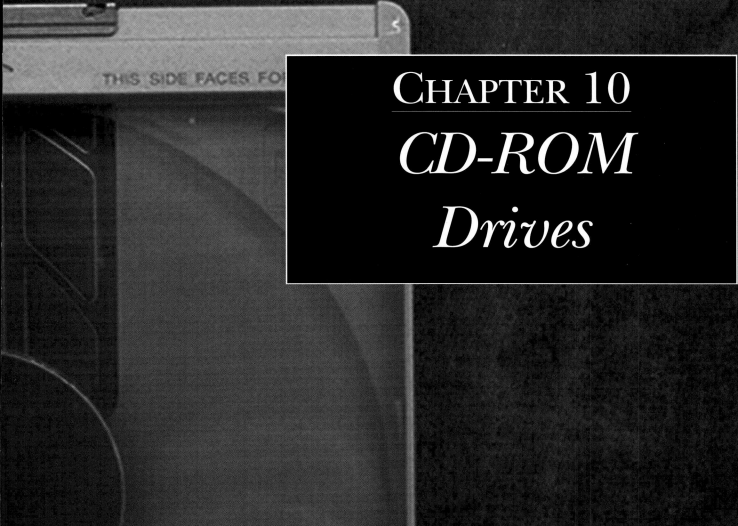

THIS SIDE FACES FO

CHAPTER 10
CD-ROM
Drives

Understanding CD-ROM Drives

CD-ROMs have their roots in the audio compact disc (CD) phenomenon of the 1980s. Audio CDs consist of a digitally recorded audio that is read by a low-power laser beam. Because there is nothing touching the actual CD, audio CDs don't wear out; this is a large improvement over earlier analog devices like albums or cassette tapes.

CD-ROMs are similar to audio CDs; they both store digital information. The only difference between the two is the type of information stored and how the CD player processes the information. Computer CD-ROMs can play music and access stored computer data. CD-ROMs have several advantages for computer users—they hold approximately 600M of information (well over twice the amount you can store on the typical hard drive), can be easily removed, and cannot be accidentally erased.

When you add a CD-ROM drive to your system, you also must install special software drivers that allow you to access the CD-ROM drive. There are two programs you will use for this purpose. One program is the actual driver supplied by the drive manufacturer; it is installed as part of your CONFIG.SYS file. The other is the MSCDEX program, which is installed as part of your AUTOEXEC.BAT file. These two programs (the driver and MSCDEX) work together to make your CD-ROM drive accessible.

Whoever supplied your CD-ROM controller card (or the sound card, if it controls your CD-ROM) should have supplied you with these two files. If they did not, contact them right away. If they did, make sure you add them to your CONFIG.SYS and AUTOEXEC.BAT files as directed in the documentation. Different CD-ROM drives and controllers require different settings for these programs. When they are installed correctly, however, you are able to access the CD-ROM drive as you would any other disk drive on your system.

Choosing a CD-ROM Drive

There are many types of CD-ROM drives. Unlike hard drives, which are sold almost exclusively as internal devices, CD-ROM drives are often purchased as external devices. The type you purchase is up to you. If your computer case is large enough, however, you may find the internal models more convenient.

There are several things you need to explore as you consider purchasing a CD-ROM drive. These items include:

- **What is the drive speed?** There are three speeds of CD-ROM drive on the market: single, double, and triple speed. In general, the faster the drive, the quicker information can be accessed by your system. Go for the fastest unit you can afford.

- **Does the unit have a carrier?** A CD-ROM is usually inserted into a carrier before it goes into the drive. You can purchase units that don't use carriers, but if the drive is to be mounted vertically instead of horizontally, make sure you get a carrier-based unit.

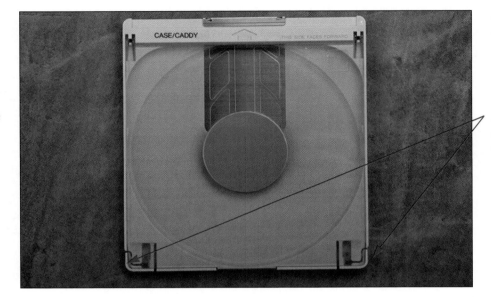

A CD-ROM carrier.

Pinch here to lift the carrier lid and insert or remove a CD-ROM.

- **Will it play audio?** Most CD-ROM drives available today also play audio CDs. While this may not seem like a big deal, many people like to listen to their favorite audio CD while they are doing other work. You can tell if the unit supports audio by whether there is a headphone jack and a volume knob on the front of the CD.

A CD-ROM drive that supports audio CDs.

Volume knob.

Headphone jack.

- **Will it play photo CDs?** Kodak recently introduced technology that enables you to put photographs on special "Photo CDs" that you can play on your computer system. If you work a lot with graphics, this is a good way to import images into programs like Adobe PhotoShop.

- **What interface does it use?** There are many different types of interfaces for CD-ROM drives. The two most common are SCSI (discussed earlier) and proprietary. Typically, proprietary interfaces are used if the CD-ROM is part of multimedia upgrade kit. In general, proprietary interfaces aren't as flexible or powerful as standard SCSI interfaces. If you already have a SCSI controller in your system, choose a CD-ROM that works with your existing SCSI controller.

REMOVING A CD-ROM DRIVE

Before removing an existing CD-ROM drive, make sure you remove any CDs that are in the drive; many of the drives on the market will only eject a CD if the power is on.

The way you remove a CD-ROM drive depends on whether it is internal or external. If it is external, you simply need to unplug it from the controller—that's it.

> **NOTE:** If you unplug an external CD-ROM drive from a SCSI controller, you may need to add a SCSI terminator on the bus. Consult the documentation for your SCSI controller for more information.

If your CD-ROM drive is an internal model, removing it is very similar to removing a hard drive or floppy drive.

1 Remove the computer case, and locate the CD-ROM drive to be removed.

Removing the screws on a CD-ROM drive.

2 On each side of the drive, there are one or two screws holding the drive securely to the drive bay. Remove these screws so you can easily slide the drive within the bay.

> **NOTE:** Depending on how your system is assembled, you may need to remove other disk drives or system components before you can get to the CD-ROM drive. If so, read the appropriate sections about removing other types of drives.

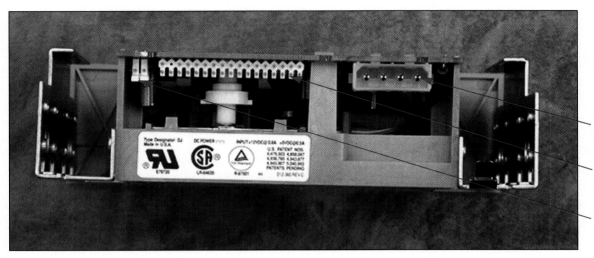

The cables connected to a CD-ROM drive: the power cable, the data cable, and the audio cable.

The power cable connects here.

The data cable connects here.

Internal audio wires connect here.

3 Look at the back of the drive, and you see that there are several different cables connected to the drive. One of these is the power cable, the other is for data, and the third (if present) is for audio. The data cable is the flat ribbon cable; remove this one now. Feel free to pull on the cable—it is strong enough. Once it is disconnected, fold the cable back out of the way so you can continue to work on the drive.

4 Remove the audio cable (if it is present). It is the smallest of the cables attached to the rear of the drive. This cable typically runs between the CD-ROM drive and a sound card. It is used when you play audio CDs through your sound card.

5 Remove the power cable. This is the one that has the four individual colored wires going into a white plug; it is the same power plug used for 5.25" disk drives. Traditionally, these types of plugs are very tight, so don't be surprised if you need to wiggle the plug in order to remove it. Just make sure you remove this cable by pulling on the plug, not on the wires.

6 If you did not remove the retaining screws all the way before you started removing cables, do so now. Once they are removed, the drive should slide freely in and out of the system.

ADDING AN INTERNAL CD-ROM DRIVE

Adding an internal CD-ROM drive to your system greatly enhances your computer's capabilities. CD-ROM drives allow you to take advantage of the vast number of CD-ROM based software. CD-ROMs give you access to on-line encyclopedias, thousands of movie clips and reviews, and in conjunction with sound boards, they can be used for interactive games and hi-tech virtual reality adventures.

> **NOTE:** If you don't have a SCSI adapter card installed in your computer, you need to add one before you can use a CD-ROM.

1 Open your computer case and decide which drive bay you want to use for the drive.

Removing the plastic panel to make room for a CD-ROM drive.

Sliding a CD-ROM drive into a drive bay.

2 You may need to remove a plastic panel from the front of the computer case in order to allow the front of the CD-ROM drive to be accessible. Normally, computer case vendors use plastic panels to cover unused drive bays. The panel may either be a part of the computer case, or part of the cover that attaches to the case. Simply use a small screwdriver to pop the panel out.

3 Slide the disk drive through the front of the computer case into the bay. Don't screw the drive in place yet; it is easier to connect the cables to the rear of the drive if you are able to slide it back and forth.

This is for the audio plug.

This is for the controller cable.

This is for the power plug.

Looking at the back of a CD-ROM drive.

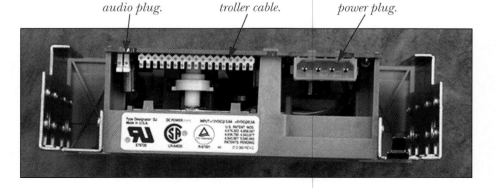

4 Connect the cables to the rear of the drive. Earlier it was mentioned that CD-ROM drives typically use three cables, whereas normal disk drives use only two. These cables are used for power, data, and audio. Begin by connecting the power cable; this is the one that has the four individual colored wires running into a white plug. Because of the way the power plug is molded, there is only one correct way to plug it in.

5 Once the power cable is connected, you can connect the controller cable. This cable runs from whatever card controls your CD-ROM drive. If you have a SCSI controller, it may run from it. If you are using an audio card or some other type of adapter card, it will run from it. Connect one end of the cable to the drive, and the other end to the controller card.

6 If you have one of the newer sound cards, you probably have a CD audio-in jack on the card. You can use a small cable to connect the audio connector on the CD-ROM drive with the connector on the sound card. This allows you, with the proper software, to play audio CDs through your sound card.

SCSI CONSIDERATIONS

If you are connecting your CD-ROM drive to a SCSI controller, you need to set the SCSI address of the CD-ROM drive. This is done either with jumpers or with switches on the CD-ROM drive. Refer to your drive documentation for information on which jumpers or switches to use. Make sure you select a device address that is different from all the others currently used in your system.

You also need to adjust SCSI terminators so they are correct for your bus configuration. Basically, the SCSI bus dictates that there be terminators at each end of the bus. In a PC system, one end of the bus is typically the controller card, with the other end being the last in your series of SCSI devices. Make sure that you remove any terminators from any other devices that are between these two bus endpoints.

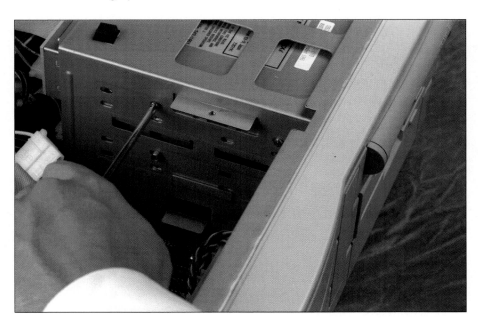

7 Now that you are through connecting cables, you can tighten the screws that hold the CD-ROM in place. Make sure you align the drive properly so that it is accessible when your computer case is back in place.

ADDING AN EXTERNAL CD-ROM DRIVE

If you have a SCSI controller card in your system, it's easy to add an external CD-ROM drive. To do so, follow these steps:

Plugging a SCSI cable into the back of an external CD-ROM drive.

1 Use a SCSI cable to plug the drive into either the back of the SCSI card or into another SCSI device. Remember that the SCSI bus allows you to daisy-chain (connect in series) devices in this manner.

> **NOTE:** If you don't have a SCSI adapter card installed in your computer, you need to add one before you can use a CD-ROM. See Chapter 4, "Inside Your PC," to find out how to insert an adapter card.

2 After you plug the drive into a SCSI port, you need to set the SCSI address of the drive. This is typically done either with jumpers or with switches on the CD-ROM drive. Refer to your drive documentation for information on which jumpers or switches to use. Make sure you select a device address which is different from all other SCSI addresses currently used in your system.

TROUBLESHOOTING CD-ROM DRIVE PROBLEMS

Adding a CD-ROM drive can add to the problems you may encounter with your computer system. First, you have to make sure everything is hooked up right. Then you have to make sure that you don't have any port conflicts, and then you have to make sure you have the right drivers loaded in the right places. If you do all that right, you'll probably be okay.

PROBLEM: My CD-ROM drive doesn't work! What am I doing wrong?

- First, do you have a CD-ROM disk inserted in the drive? Properly (label side up)? If you're using an external drive, is it powered up? Chances are this problem is caused by a bad or disconnected power cable to your CD-ROM. Check all the cables in your installation.

PROBLEM: Okay, I got the drive to spin, but I can't seem to read the disk. What's wrong now?

- The first thing to check is the drivers for your CD-ROM drive. Are they loaded in memory (via the AUTOEXEC.BAT and CONFIG.SYS files)? If so, you might want to check to see if they're loaded into high memory. If so, change the commands to load them into conventional memory. Finally, check for IRQ, DMA, and other port conflicts.

PROBLEM: My drive is spinning, and then it froze my system! Come on, what's going on here?

- Well, this is almost certainly caused by a DMA, IRQ, or port conflict. Change some assignments and see what happens.

PROBLEM: My CD-ROM works, but I can't get sound through my speakers. You hear what I'm saying?

- First, make sure you have the right drivers loaded for both your CD-ROM drive and your sound card; then make sure you have your CD-ROM drive hooked up to your sound card, and that you have your external speakers hooked up and turned on. If all else fails, it's possible that your CD-ROM drive and your sound card are incompatible. Believe it or not, some sound cards won't work with some CD-ROM drives. Check with the manufacturers of your equipment for a solution.

PROBLEM: When I stuck my latest Rolling Stones CD in the CD-ROM drive, nothing happened. Got any ideas?

- As much as we all like listening to the Rolling Stones, an audio CD cannot be played in a CD-ROM drive without the presence of special software. Such software is typically provided with your sound card or with the CD-ROM drive.

CHAPTER 11
Tape Drives

UNDERSTANDING TAPE DRIVES

As hard drives get bigger and bigger, more and more people are finding it a real pain to make backups of their data on floppy disks. Consider that backing up 300M of data can take about 30 floppy disks, and you can see why someone doesn't want to take an afternoon doing a backup.

This is where tape backups come in handy. These devices allow you to back up to 25G (that's gigabytes) of data on a single tape. With the proper type of tape drive, you could suck up the data in your entire town onto a single tape. (What an awesome sense of power!) With some types of backup software, you can set your system to do unattended backups at night or on weekends.

For the PC world, there are two major types of tape drives. Each uses a different type of tape, and each uses a different recording technology. The first type is the quarter-inch tape format, and the other is the helical scan format.

Quarter-Inch Tape Drives

Quarter-inch tape drives are generally divided into two types: DC2000 and DC6000. Both types use tape that is one-quarter inch wide, although the tape is held in different size cartridges.

A tape cartridge for a DC2000 tape drive.

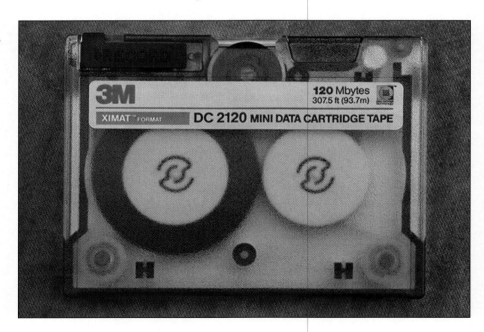

The DC2000 and DC6000 drives differ in their internal mechanisms and in the speed at which they can read or write data. To allow higher throughput, for example, the DC6000 drives use two heads. This allows them to format the tape as your data is being backed up. On the DC2000 drives, such a process requires separate passes of the tape.

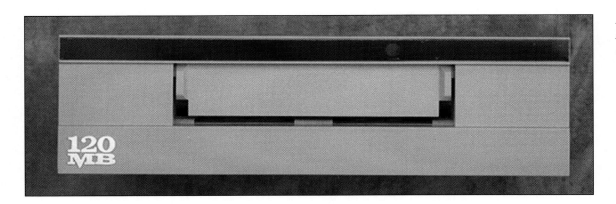

A 120M capacity DC2000 tape drive.

Information is written to the tape in any number of different formats. Regardless of whether your drive is a DC2000 or DC6000, these formats are decided upon by an industry committee called the QIC (quarter-inch committee). You can tell what type of format a drive implements by looking for the letters QIC followed by a number. For instance, drives that follow the QIC-80 format allow you to backup as much as 80M of uncompressed data.

Tape drives that use quarter-inch tape can store up to several gigabytes of information, with the most common formats allowing for 250M of information. Drives at this capacity can be purchased for as little as $200, and they can be controlled by your floppy disk controller (although dedicated controllers also are available for an additional cost).

Helical Scan Tape Drives

Tape drives in this category use a radically different method of storing information on tape. The helical scan method involves physically wrapping the tape around a revolving head, but wrapping it at a skewed angle. The quarter-inch formats described in the previous section allow for the tape to pass by stationary heads.

There are two types of helical scan tape drives. One is the 8mm tape drives, and the other is the 4mm DAT (digital audio tape) drives. The 8mm drives are the more expensive, but they also generally allow for greater speed and storage capacity. These drives use technology that is an offshoot of the Betamax VCR technology developed in the 1970s.

The 4mm DAT drives use technology that was developed for digital audio tape players, which never quite made it in the electronics world. These drives offer large capacity with a small tape size. (The tapes are only about 3" by 2" and only ⅜" thick.)

One of the drawbacks to helical scan tape drives is that they are typically more expensive than the quarter-inch tape drives. Good DAT drives, which cost less than 8mm drives, still start at more than $1,000 dollars. While that may sound like quite a bit, it is a small price to pay if you have large amounts of data to back up and you want to do it unattended. This scenario virtually dictates that you go for the larger capacity drives.

REMOVING AN INTERNAL TAPE DRIVE

The procedure for removing an internal tape drive is straightforward. The next several steps show you how to remove a tape drive:

1 Begin by removing the computer case, and then locate the drive you want removed.

The tape drive's data cable.

The tape drive's power cable.

The mounting screws on a tape drive.

2 Loosen the mounting screws on both sides of the drive, so you can slide the drive forward and backward in the drive bay.

NOTE: Depending on how your system has been assembled, you may need to remove other disk drives or system components before you can get to the tape drive. If you need to, read the sections on upgrading floppy and hard disk drives in chapters 8 and 9 for pointers on how to remove other system components.

The data and power cables on the back of a tape drive.

3 Pull the tape drive forward in the bay to allow as much workroom behind the drive as possible. Notice that there are two cables attached to the back of the drive. One is for power, and the other for data. Remove the data cable first; this is the flat ribbon cable. Simply grab the cable and firmly pull it out of the connector on the back of the drive. Pulling on the cable will not harm the cable or the connector. Fold the cable back out of the way so that you can continue to work on the drive.

4 The power cable is the one that has the four individual colored wires going into a white plug. Removing this cable is sometimes more challenging than removing the data cable—the plug generally fits in the connector very snugly. As you wiggle the plug to free it from the connector, make sure you pull on the plug, not on the wires.

5 Now that the cables are removed, you can completely undo the retaining screws on both sides of the tape drive.

NOTE: If your system's data and power cables are long enough, you can slide the drive completely out of the case before you remove the cables. Doing so makes reaching the cables more convenient that trying to disconnect the cables inside a cramped computer case.

The tape drive out of the drive bay.

6 Once the retaining screws are removed, you can pull the tape drive out the front of the drive bay and set it aside.

7 You still have one other step to perform before the drive can be considered fully removed. This involves the cable and (possibly) the controller. If you take another look at the data cable you removed from the back of the tape drive, notice that it leads somewhere (good thing, right?). Exactly where it leads will depend on the type of interface you are using.

If you are using the lower cost quarter-inch tape drives, there is a good chance that the cable leads to the cable going between your floppy drives and the disk controller. Alternatively, it could lead to a dedicated tape drive controller. The third option (if you are using a helical scan tape drive) is that it leads to your SCSI controller, which also controls other devices in your system. Regardless of where it leads, the cable needs to be removed. Unplug it from where it leads, and then store the cable with the tape drive.

8 If you were using a dedicated tape drive controller, you also can remove it from your system. If you ran the tape drive off of a SCSI controller, you may need to adjust the terminators on the SCSI bus.

ADDING AN INTERNAL TAPE DRIVE

Regardless of the type of internal tape drive you are installing, the process is the same.

1 Start by taking the cover off of your computer and identify where you want the tape drive placed. Select a drive bay that is large enough to hold your tape drive. Depending on the type of drive you select, you could almost fit them anywhere; some of the 4mm DAT drives can even be placed in a 3.5" drive bay.

2 If necessary, remove any plastic cover in the computer case that may block access to the tape drive when you are through with your installation. These can easily be popped out with a small screwdriver.

3 Remove the tape drive from its packaging and slide it into the front of the drive bay. Don't secure it with screws yet; it is easier to connect the cables if you wait on this step.

The power cable and plug to use with a tape drive.

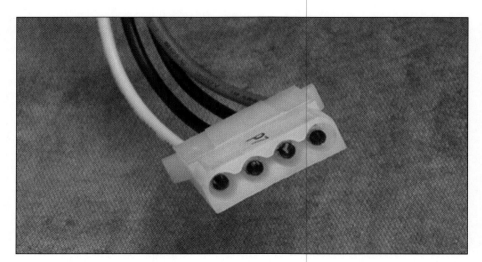

4 Instead, slide the drive in far enough that you can connect the power cable. This is the small white plastic connector at the end of four colored wires. It is the same type of power plug used on the 5.25" disk drives. Because of the way the power plug is designed, there is only one way to insert it firmly in the power connector.

Looking at the back of a typical tape drive.

This is for the controller cable.

This is for the power cable.

NOTE: Not all tape drives appear as shown in this picture. Instead, they may have a bit different configuration. The important thing is that you identify and use the proper connectors for both power and data.

---

5 Once you have connected the power cable, you can attach the controller cable. Plug one end of the cable into the proper connector on the rear of the drive, and the other end into the proper controller location. There are three types of controller connections your drive could use, depending on what type it is.

- *Connected to a SCSI controller.* In this case, make sure you also configure any SCSI terminators necessary and set any device addresses that are needed by the controller.

- *Connected to a dedicated controller.* This is easy. Simply connect the cable plug to the connector on the controller.

- *Connected through a floppy disk controller.* This is done by removing the floppy controller cable and adding the tape drive controller cable. The floppy controller cable then plugs into a connector on the tape drive cable. This method of connecting a tape drive is very common with lower-price tape drives.

6 You are now ready to start using your tape drive. All you need to do is put your computer back together and start it up. Remember that you cannot access a tape drive as you would other disk drives or CD-ROMs on your system. Instead, you must use special backup software that allows you to directly address the tape drive.

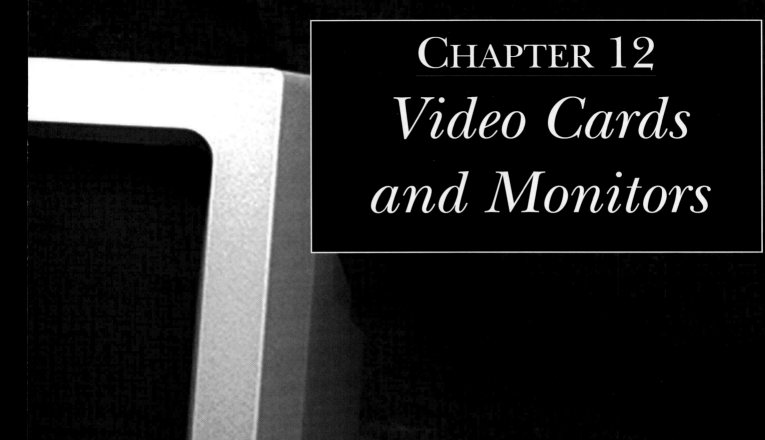

CHAPTER 12
Video Cards and Monitors

Understanding Your Video System

Your video system is actually made up of two distinct parts—a video card and a monitor. These pieces work together to provide your output. The video card controls the display you see on-screen; the monitor controls the crispness and quality of what is displayed.

Without a good video card, a good monitor will not provide satisfying results. Conversely, without a good monitor, the capabilities of a good video card will be stifled. It is important that both elements be matched close in capability and features so you can get the best possible display.

Understanding Video Cards

Over the years there have been many different types of video standards that have come and gone. When anyone talks about video standards, they are typically referring to the way in which information is displayed by a video card. There have been six distinct video standards, each with their own capabilities:

- **Monochrome Display Adapter (MDA).** The earliest available type of PC display, the MDA provided a text-only display; there was no graphics capability. It presented text in a single color in the familiar 80-character by 25-line display.

- **Color Graphics Adapter (CGA).** The CGA was the first color video card on the market. It featured 16-color text displays or two graphics displays: four colors at a resolution of 320 by 200 pixels or two colors at a resolution of 640 by 400 pixels.

- **Enhanced Graphics Adapter (EGA).** The EGA display system was a huge step up in quality from the earlier CGA. It could display 16-color graphics at a resolution of 640 by 350 pixels. In addition, programmers could create custom fonts that displayed in graphics mode, thus enabling the creation of the first true WYSIWYG (what you see is what you get) displays.

- **Video Graphics Array (VGA).** Introduced in 1987, VGA featured the ability to completely emulate earlier video standards, as well as display up to 256 colors from more than 262,144 choices. Resolutions also were improved, to a maximum of 640 by 480 pixels.

- **Extended Graphics Array (XGA).** The XGA (or the subsequent XGA/2) is not a video standard for all PC systems, because IBM only offers it for the MCA bus. Both cards offer superior performance to the VGA, meaning speed in displaying information. They also up the resolution to 1,024 by 768 pixels with 256 colors, or 640 by 480 pixels with 65,536 colors.

- **Super VGA (SVGA).** This isn't a standard per se, but rather a way of identifying systems that go beyond that of standard VGA. For example, one card may offer higher resolution, while another offers more colors, and a third may offer both. These cards collectively form a class known as SVGA. This is not a real video standard, however, since each vendor offers different capabilities; there is no real measuring stick.

A pixel is a term meaning picture element. It represents a single addressable point of light on the display screen. The number of pixels that can be displayed on a monitor defines the monitor's video resoultion.

A 16-bit video card.

> **NOTE:** The video card determines the speed and displayable resolution of your display. Many video cards support more than one resolution—some may be greater than your monitor can display and others may be lower. Make certain the capabilities of your video card and monitor are well matched.

In addition to video resolution, it's important to note the speed that your video display is refreshed. There are many ways you can improve the speed at which your video adapter displays information. They are:

- **Video coprocessor.** A CPU on the video card that relieves your main CPU of the time-consuming tasks associated with displaying video.

- **Video RAM (VRAM).** A special type of memory chip, which is optimized for video systems.

- **Local Bus (VL-Bus).** A special-purpose bus, used primarily for video, that allows fast transfer of video data at the full width and speed of your main data bus.

Understanding Monitors

There are literally hundreds (if not thousands) of different monitors on the market, and each of them seem to have different specifications. The following six items should be considered when you decide to buy a new monitor:

- **Image Size.** There are a wide range of monitor sizes available, with 14-, 15-, 17-, and 21-inch measurements being the most common. (Image size is measured diagonally, not including the monitor's case.) You should get a monitor size that allows you to view your work in comfort. In general, the higher the resolution, the larger the screen size you will want to use.

- **Screen Technology.** The display tubes in the monitor can either be curved (which is what you normally see in your TV) or flat screen. For picture quality, viewing comfort, and reducing glare, flat screens are best.

- **Dot Pitch.** This is a technical term referring to the distance between individual dots (pixels) on the screen. The lower the dot pitch, the smoother the image appears. Dot pitches range anywhere between 0.25mm and 0.45mm, with the lower numbers being better. For a good monitor, you want a dot pitch of 0.28mm or less.

- **Scanning Frequency.** Often called the refresh rate, this refers to how quickly the electron guns within the monitor can update the image on-screen. How quickly the guns move horizontally is called the horizontal scan rate, and how quickly they move down the screen is called the vertical scan rate. You want a monitor that has a high refresh rate; the higher the rate, the less flicker you will see in the images produced. Make sure the scan rates produced by your video card can be matched by the monitor you are considering. Mismatched rates can cause improper displays and also can physically damage your monitor.

- **Interlacing.** This refers to how the monitor "paints" the image on-screen. Interlaced monitors display alternate rows of pixels as the electron guns move down the screen; first the odd, and then the even. Non-interlaced monitors don't skip any rows; they all are displayed sequentially. The non-interlaced monitors provide the highest quality display.

- **Phosphor Persistence.** On the inside of the tube in your monitor is a thin coating of a substance called phosphor. This chemical, when electrically charged, emits a glow. That is what creates the images you see on-screen—the glow from the phosphor being charged by the electron guns in the back of the tube. Persistence refers to how long the phosphor remains glowing after the charge is removed. Persistence is important because if it is too low, you will see flicker; if it is too high, you will see ghosts. It is important to ascertain whether there is a good match between the phosphor and the scanning frequency of your monitor.

CHOOSING A VIDEO SYSTEM

Now comes the hard part—you need to pick your video system. The choices available are bewildering at times, but hopefully the information presented so far will help you along. The following guidelines should help:

- Pick a video card that provides the greatest number of features your budget will allow. Look for high resolution and a great number of colors (65,536 or more).

- Choose the fastest video card possible. Look for one that combines a VRAM, a video coprocessor, and VL-Bus technology. (You may have to leave off the VL-Bus stipulation if your motherboard does not have a local bus slot.)

- Pick a monitor that will easily support the high-resolution video signals generated by your video card. Look for one with a flat screen, low dot pitch, a fast refresh rate, and accessible controls.

- Visit a computer dealer to see the capabilities of the video system in action. If there is no computer dealer close by, visit a friend who may already have invested in the system you are considering.

> **NOTE:** Remember that if you are purchasing a complete computer system, the video card and monitors bundled into these package deals are often minimal systems. It would be well worth your time to upgrade, right from the start, to a video system that will give you the performance you want.

TROUBLESHOOTING VIDEO PROBLEMS

Most video problems can be traced to bad connections, so make sure all your cables are firmly plugged in. Also make sure that you have installed the correct drivers for your video setup, and that your driver's are the most recent version. Finally, it's possible that you have a video card/monitor combination that doesn't work together; when in doubt, check with the manufacturer.

PROBLEM: My monitor is dead! What's wrong?

- First, check the power cable to the monitor. (You might as well make sure the wall switch is turned on, while you're at it!) Next, check the cable from the monitor to the video card. Then check the video card itself; make sure it's seated properly. Finally, check your documentation and see if there are any switches on your video card or motherboard that you have to set to make this card work.

PROBLEM: My monitor seems to display only one color all of a sudden. I sort of like the green hue, but is it supposed to do that color?

- There are typically two causes for this sort of condition. First (and most likely), your monitor cable is loose. Check the back of the PC to make sure that the monitor cable is secure, and then reboot your machine. If the cable was loose, this will correct the problem.

  The other possible cause, although not quite as likely, is that you have had something happen to either the video card or the monitor that has caused one or two of the video signals to not get through. Every monitor works by firing a red, blue, or green electron gun at just the right time to create the images you see. If any of those guns don't fire, that color is missing from the image. If you suspect this problem, plug the monitor into someone else's computer to see if it works there. If it does, it is your video card. If it still doesn't work, take the monitor to a reputable repair business.

PROBLEM: The monitor makes this terrible high-pitched sound when I turn it on. What would cause that?

- It typically means that one of the electronic components within the monitor is on the verge of going out. However, the monitor could continue functioning for quite some time. Problem is, how long do you want to continue putting up with the irritating high-pitch whine? The only solution is to take the monitor to a repair depot.

PROBLEM: All of my software seems to run fine with my new video card, except for Windows. How come?

- The best bet is to make sure Windows is set to use a regular, generic VGA driver; this should make it work right away. The problem is that you can't use the high-resolution modes of your card this way. Contact your card vendor to see if there are drivers available that will allow the card to be used with Windows.

REMOVING YOUR OLD VIDEO SYSTEM

The first thing you should do when you want to remove a video system is to start all your software programs that have special video drivers and reset them to a default video card. If you use Windows, and you are using a special video driver for the video card you are removing, then you should open the Control Panel, go to System Setup, and set your video driver back to plain old VGA.

> **CAUTION:** If you don't reset your video drivers, you may not be able to use the software with whatever new video system you install. In fact, you won't even be able to load the software to change to the new driver. Make certain you reset them so that they work with the new video card.

There are two parts to removing a video system:

1 Disconnect and remove the monitor. All you need to do is unplug it from the wall and from the back of your PC.

Removing an old video card.

2 Next, you will need to open your computer system and remove the video card. (You can identify which one it is because you just disconnected the monitor from it, right?)

ADDING YOUR NEW VIDEO CARD

When installing a new video card, make sure you read all the documentation that came with the card. This is important because, invariably, there will be switches you need to set for the card to work properly with your monitor.

Here is how to install a new video card:

Expansion slots on a motherboard.

High speed local bus slots.

Regular slots.

1 Open your computer case and select the slot where you want the card inserted. If possible, pick a slot that is distanced from other cards on the board.

2 If you are installing a local bus video card, make sure you select the proper slot for the card. You can identify the slot by its size; local bus slots are larger than regular slots.

3 If there is a slot cover at the rear of the computer case, where the external part of the adapter card will be situated, remove the cover. If you are unsure how to remove a slot cover, see Chapter 4, "Inside Your PC."

Sliding a video card into its slot.

Local bus connector.

4 Slide the adapter card straight down into the slot. The rear of the adapter card should slide into the slot at the rear of the computer case, and the edge connector should seat firmly in the slot on the motherboard. You may need to apply a bit of downward pressure to firmly seat the adapter card.

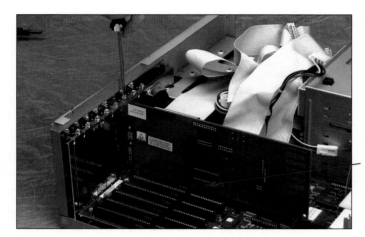

Fastening the retaining screw.

The card firmly seated in the slot.

5 Once the card is fully seated within the adapter card slot, replace the retaining screw so it secures the adapter card in place.

Connecting the monitor cable to the video card.

6 Now you need to connect your monitor cable to the video card. Even though many cards have two connectors, you will find that it's easy to identify the connector for your particular monitor cable.

ADDING YOUR NEW MONITOR

Before you connect your new monitor to your video card, you may need to put it together. Strange as it may sound, some monitors require a little assembly before they can be used. Typically, this is nothing more than connecting the monitor base to the actual monitor case.

As an example, take a look at the monitor shown in the accompanying pictures. This monitor actually started as two pieces—the base and the monitor.

A typical PC video monitor.

The monitor. —

The monitor base. —

Most monitors ship with the base separated from the monitor. To learn how to attach the base to your monitor, use these steps:

Slots to connect the monitor base.

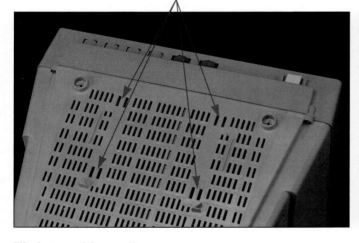

The bottom of the monitor case.

Hooks to connect with the monitor case.

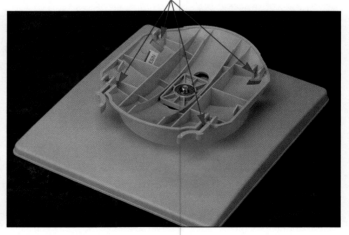

The monitor base.

1 When assembling a monitor, you usually have the best luck if you turn it upside down. When you do, notice the slots in the bottom of the monitor into which you can connect the base. These slots are designed to hold hooks in the monitor base.

2 Position the monitor base so that the hooks fall into the slots in the monitor case.

*Slide the base backward
to lock it to the case.*

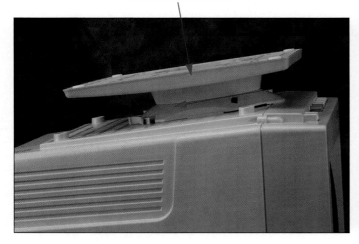

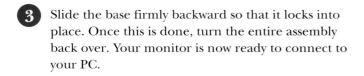

Putting the monitor and monitor base together.

The plug on the end of a video cable.

3 Slide the base firmly backward so that it locks into place. Once this is done, turn the entire assembly back over. Your monitor is now ready to connect to your PC.

4 To connect the monitor to your PC, simply plug the video cable into the connector on the back of the video card. Most monitors available today use a male 15-pin connector. This plug is inserted into the corresponding connector on the back of the video card. Video cables are rather sturdy because of their shielding, so firmly attach the plug with the connector by using the retaining screws on the plug.

5 Now you can connect the power cord on the monitor. There are two styles of plugs you can get. One connects your monitor directly to a wall outlet, and the other is used to connect the monitor to a power outlet on the back of your PC. You don't see much of this latter type any more, but they are still available. You can tell them apart simply because it is impossible to plug the latter type of power connector into your wall.

6 You have now installed your video system and you are ready to test it. The best way to test your system is to turn it on. If all elements are connected correctly, your system should boot right up and you should see video information on-screen.

Tip: What if you don't see anything on-screen about the time you start hearing the normal booting sounds come from your PC (you know—the clicks, hums, and whirrs that you typically hear but take for granted)? First, make certain that the power plug is firmly inserted into the monitor and plugged in to the wall. Next, confirm that the monitor is turned on—look for the little green light on the front panel. Finally, try turning the brightness and contrast knobs.

UNDERSTANDING SOUND AND MULTIMEDIA

In recent years, one buzzword has popped up again and again in the press—multimedia. At its simplest, multimedia means the combination of video and audio (pictures and sound) often stored on a CD-ROM disc.

One of the key elements of multimedia—one that is present in virtually every presentation—is audio. In the PC environment, audio capability is added to a PC through a sound card and speakers.

Sound cards add a dimension to computing that few people appreciate until they work with a system that utilizes sound well. By adding a sound card, you can use software designed to entertain or educate in a variety of ways. If you fancy yourself as a musician, you can even add MIDI capabilities, which allow you to compose and play back compositions on your PC.

The cheapest sound cards are those primarily intended for use with games. These cards are usually compatible with the original AdLib card—the first really popular sound card.

The next level of sound cards are the cards that are intended for use in making real music. These type of sound cards are typically used to control MIDI devices, like keyboards or synthesizers, or to play files created on MIDI compatible devices.

The popular Sound Blaster sound card kit.

There are many cards on the market that provide sound for both games and MIDI. The most well-known of these are the Sound Blaster family of cards. These cards, while they tout themselves as being a "card for all purposes," typically do the games sound very well, but don't quite measure up to professional standards on the MIDI side.

TROUBLESHOOTING AUDIO PROBLEMS

Multimedia setups can cause problems because they're so complex. In addition to the normal devices hooked up to your PC (such as your printer, mouse, keyboard, and monitor), you now have a CD-ROM drive, sound card, and a set of external speakers. This is a lot of stuff to get hooked up and configured right; because of this, most multimedia problems are setup problems.

PROBLEM: I just installed my sound card and now another device on my system won't work. Could the sound card be causing this?

- Probably. If the I/O address, interrupts, and DMA channels used by the sound card are the same as those used by other adapter cards in your system, neither the sound card nor the other adapter will work properly. Check all your settings and try again.

PROBLEM: Nope. Can't get a peep out of it. It worked one time; why not now?

- Check your speaker wires. There is a good chance that one of them got pulled out. Then make sure you have the speaker plug in the proper jack on the back of the sound card. If that still doesn't work, make sure that no other software you are using has changed the settings used by the sound card. Another option you may want to check is the volume knob to see that it is at the proper level.

PROBLEM: I finally got the card working, but the sound is intermittent. Why does it sound like the music is skipping?

- This problem generally results from an IRQ conflict. Change the interrupt setting for your sound card to one not used by another system device and then reboot your system.

PROBLEM: My setup seems to be working, except I'm only getting sound from one speaker. Am I going deaf, or what?

- No, it's not you, it may be the plug on your speakers. When you use a mono plug with stereo speakers, you only get half the sound. Try using the right kind of plug for your speaker connections, and also check the driver for your sound card.

PROBLEM: My system's sound plays too fast! How do I slow things down?

- Some computers are just too fast for certain sound cards. In many cases you can change sound drivers or "turbo down" your computer to run at a slower speed. It's also possible that your PC and your sound card just aren't compatible.

INSTALLING A SOUND CARD

Since there are dozens of different sound cards on the market, it would be impossible to list all of the installation steps and nuances for each individual card. It is, however, possible to provide an example that you can apply to your particular situation. The discussion in the next several sections assumes you are going to install a Sound Blaster 16, a 16-bit version of one of the largest selling sound cards on the market.

To install a Sound Blaster 16, follow these steps:

The jumper locations for setting base addresses.

Used to set the regular sound card I/O address.

Used to set the MIDI chip I/O address.

1 Begin by setting the base addresses used by the Sound Blaster 16. A base address or an I/O port is used by software to communicate with the card. There are two different I/O port base addresses you need to set. The first is for regular sound card operations, and the other is for MIDI use. You set these using jumpers on the card itself. These two jumpers control the four possible I/O port address settings. The table *Jumper settings for Sound Blaster 16 ASP I/O port addresses* lists the possible settings for the jumpers.

JUMPER SETTINGS FOR SOUND BLASTER 16 ASP I/O PORT ADDRESSES.

I/O Port	Jumper IOS0	Jumper IOS1	
220h	closed	closed	
240h	open	closed	
260h	closed	open	
280h	open	open	

> **NOTE:** Under normal circumstances, you should not have to make changes to the default I/O address settings. An exception is if there are other adapter cards in your system that already use the default addresses used by the Sound Blaster 16. Notice, however, that the Sound Blaster 16 allows you to set several parameters through configuration software provided with your sound card.

2 Locate a slot on your motherboard for your Sound Blaster card.

3 If there is a slot cover at the rear of the computer case, where the external part of the Sound Blaster card will be situated, remove the cover.

Sliding an adapter card into its slot.

4 Slide the Sound Blaster card straight down into the slot. The rear of the card should slide into the slot at the rear of the computer case, and the edge connector should seat firmly in the slot on the motherboard. You may need to apply a bit of downward pressure to firmly seat the adapter card.

5 Once the card is fully seated within the adapter card slot, replace the retaining screw so it secures the adapter card in place.

Connectors on the back of a sound card.

This is the microphone connector.

This is the external speaker connector.

This is the joystick/MIDI connector.

6 If you want to connect a microphone to your Sound Blaster card, plug the microphone plug into the jack on the rear of the sound card.

7 To connect an MIDI device, plug a connecting cable into the card and then into the MIDI device.

CD-ROM connectors on the Sound Blaster 16.

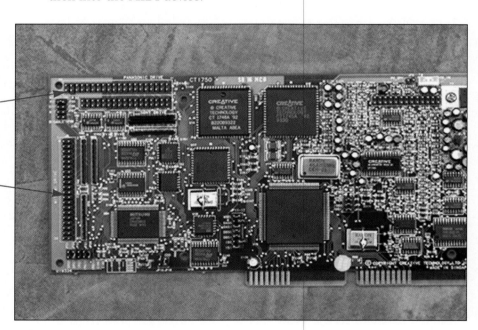

A connector used to control Panasonic CD-ROM drives.

A connector used to control Mitsumi CD-ROM drives.

8 One of the biggest additions to many sound cards is the capability to control CD-ROM drives. Run the controller cable from the CD-ROM drive to the appropriate connector on the sound card.

NOTE: Typically a sound card will support only a single or limited number of CD-ROM drives. Your best bet might be to buy a multimedia upgrade kit that contains a matched sound card and CD-ROM drive.

9 After the CD-ROM controller cable is connected, you also can connect an audio cable between the sound card and the CD-ROM drive. This allows you to record music from audio CDs or to play them back through your system.

Securing the sound card.

10 When all these devices are connected, fasten the card securely to your system unit and proceed to the next step—installing speakers.

INSTALLING SPEAKERS

The following instructions will work for almost any brand of external speakers.

Connections on the back of a Sound Blaster 16.

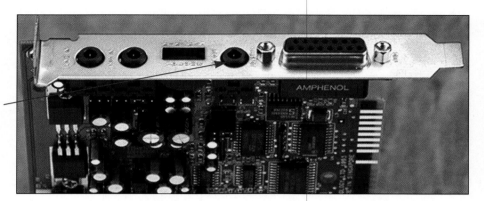

This is the speaker output jack.

On the back of your sound card is a speaker connection. Virtually every sound card on the market uses a jack for a stereo ⅛" mini-plug for their speaker connections. Thus, your speakers should use this type of plug. This is great if you have small speakers, like those for a personal stereo; you can plug them in directly. These smaller speakers are inexpensive and easy to plug in.

A set of small speakers which can be used with a PC.

A better alternative is to connect the output from your sound card to the auxiliary inputs of your home stereo system. In order to do this, however, you will need to get an adapter from your local electronic supply store. This is because the output on your sound card requires a stereo ⅛" mini-plug while your home stereo system typically requires RCA phono plugs for input. Recognizing how common this approach to PC sound is, some sound card vendors supply the appropriate adapter with the sound card.

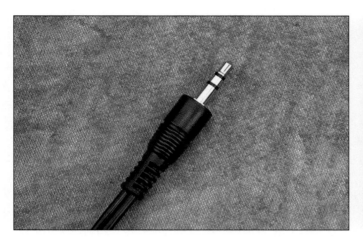

An ⅛" stereo mini-plug.

RCA phono plugs for left (white) and right (red) channels.

The best approach to providing quality sound for your sound card is to use self-powered speakers. These include their own amplifiers that help boost the amplitude of what is created by the sound card. There are a variety of these types of speakers on the market, and they run the gamut in price, from as little as $35 a pair to more than $750 a pair.

> **CAUTION:** All high-quality speakers include magnets that create the sound you hear. If you purchase speakers that will be used in a computer environment—particularly those that will be placed on each side of your monitor—make sure they are well shielded. The shielding helps protect the monitor from the effects of the magnets, which can distort an image and damage a monitor.

TELLING SOFTWARE ABOUT YOUR SOUND CARD

Different software will tap into the power of your sound card in different ways. Some software will automatically detect and use a sound card. Other software must be configured to recognize the sound card.

You won't need to do any work with those programs that automatically detect and use the sound card; it will just happen. If you need to manually configure your software, refer to your documentation to determine which commands or programs do the actual configuration. When you are asked to select your type of sound card, it is possible you won't be able to find your card on the list. In these cases, select the name of a sound card your's will emulate. If you still are not sure which one to use, select the AdLib card. Virtually every piece of software that supports sound cards will support the AdLib card.

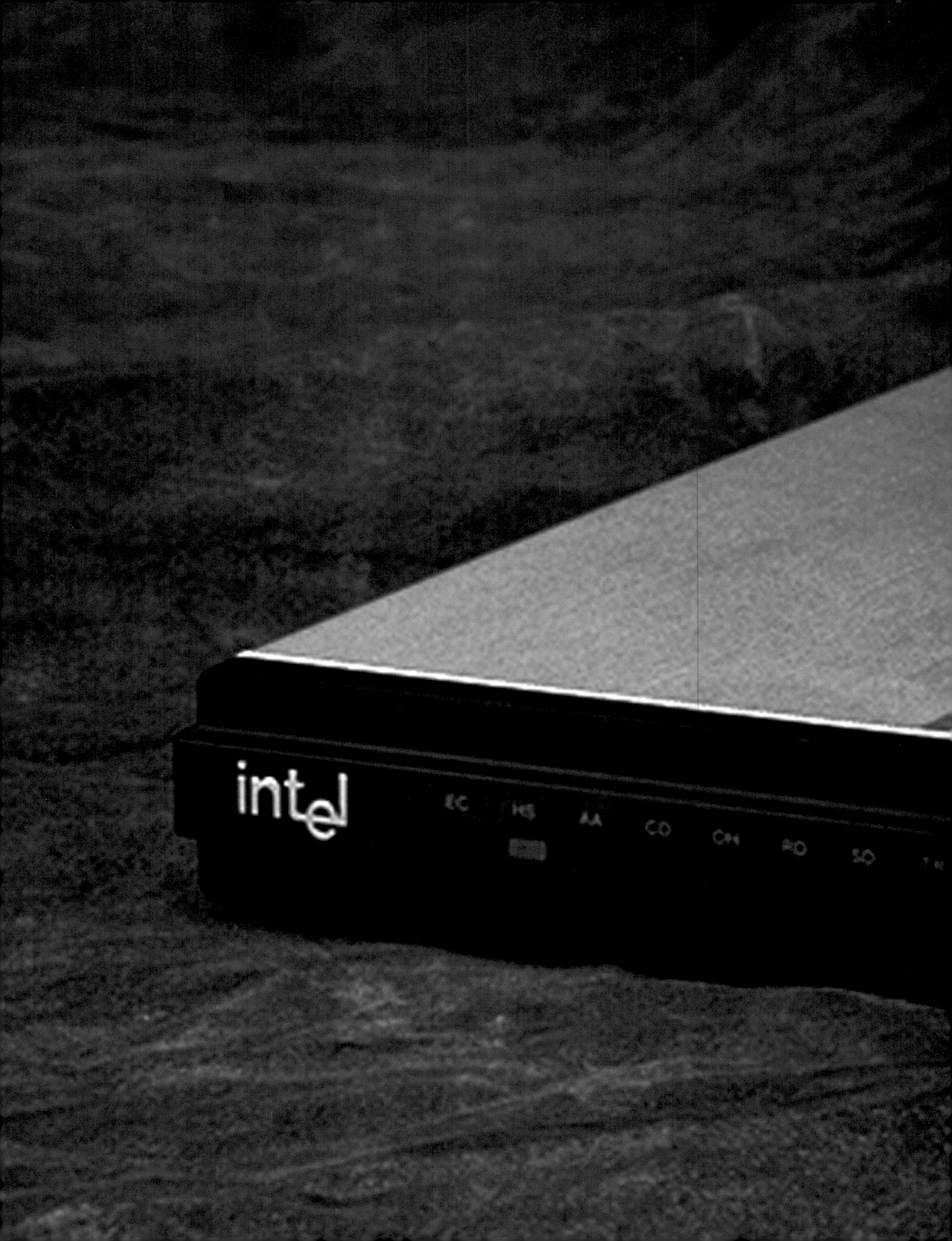
intel
EC
HS
AA
CD
OH
RD
SD

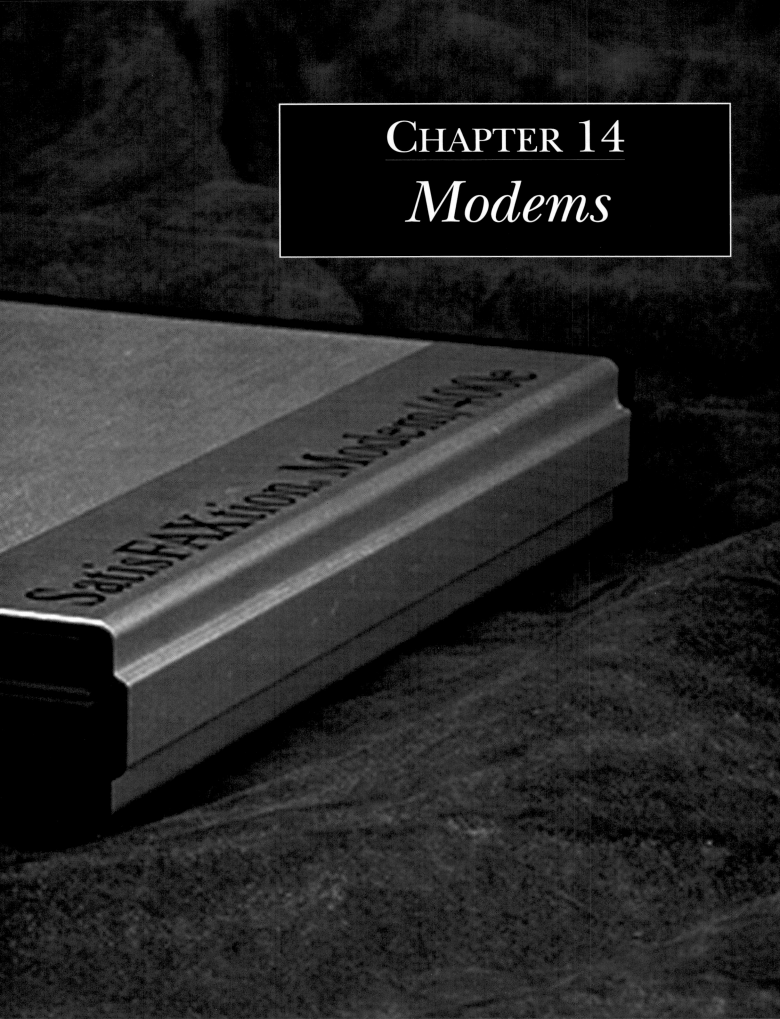

CHAPTER 14
Modems

UNDERSTANDING MODEMS

Technically speaking, the term *modem* is a contraction meaning *modulate/demodulate.* This describes the process that a modem goes through—it turns digital data into analog information which can be transmitted over a phone line; this is the modulate part. Demodulation occurs at the far end of the connection where another modem reverses the process and converts the analog signal back into digital information the computer can understand.

How data is transmitted over phone lines.

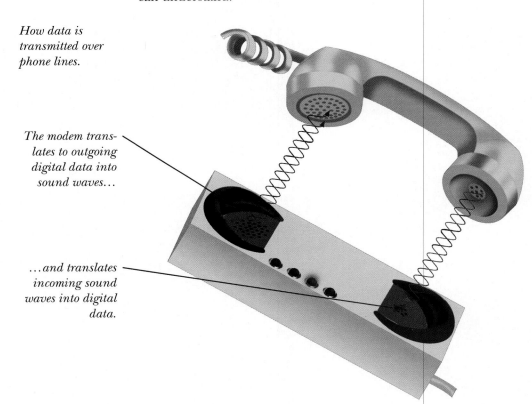

The modem translates to outgoing digital data into sound waves...

...and translates incoming sound waves into digital data.

Why is this conversion to and from an analog signal necessary? Quite simply because our telephone system is built around analog technology. It literally carries sound waves (in electronic form) across the wires. This is a simple effective way to carry conversations, but it does computers no good. Thus, modems are needed.

There are two ways to send information across a phone line. The first is synchronous transmission, in which data arrives at precisely timed intervals. In fact, there is a timing signal that is constantly transmitted over the connection. This helps keep information from getting bunched up at one end of the link.

Asynchronous communication, on the other hand, is less structured. In this arrangement, data can be sent at the leisure of the transmitting party and received thereafter by the receiving party. No timing signal is necessary in this arrangement.

Synchronous transmission is similar to the railroad. Each car of the train is precisely a set distance from every other car. When the train arrives at the destination, it is received and processed one car at a time. The track helps to make sure that the cars don't bunch up. (Can you think of a single train in which, during an uninterrupted trip—the transmission, if you will—the cars arrived at the destination in a different order from which they left?)

Asynchronous communication can be likened to our freeway systems. The messages (the cars) travel to the destination at no set interval. There can be any manner of gap in between the cars as they depart.

Why use one type of transmission over another? Simple. Synchronous communication is capable of higher transmission speeds with less overhead—the timing signal helps keep things straight. When you transmit data in an asynchronous fashion, extra bits must be placed around each packet of information (each byte) that allows the receiving modem to "get in step," so it can receive the data properly. On the other hand, asynchronous communication is typically cheaper and more appropriate to dial-up communication over ordinary telephone lines, while synchronous communication is used over dedicated phone lines between large computer systems.

STANDARD PC IRQ SETTINGS.

STANDARD PC IRQ SETTINGS.

IRQ	Purpose
0	System timer
1	Keyboard controller
2	Cascade to second IRQ controller (8 through 15)
3	Serial port 2 (COM2:)
4	Serial port 1 (COM1:)
5	Parallel port 2 (LPT2:)
6	Floppy disk controller
7	Parallel port 1 (LPT1:)
8	Real-time clock
9	Unused
10	Unused
11	Unused
12	Motherboard mouse port
13	Math coprocessor (NPX)
14	Hard disk controller
15	Unused

UNDERSTANDING COM PORTS

Your modem needs to know which serial communications port (also called a COM port) you want it to use. In older PC systems, you could use either COM1 or COM2; newer systems sold today also allow you to use either COM3 or COM4.

If you are installing an external modem, you can pick either COM1 or COM2, since these are the ports usually provided with your PC. If you are installing an internal modem, you will need to set switches on your modem board that tell the modem what COM port it should use.

When selecting a COM port, particularly for an internal modem, there is one thing to keep in mind. If you have a system based on the ISA bus, you should not use a serial device on COM1 and COM3 at the same time, nor should you use devices on COM2 and COM4 at the same time. Why? Because if you do, you will confuse your PC. (This confusion does not exist if you are using an EISA or MCA bus computer.)

Take another look at the interrupt table for a PC. Notice that there are only two COM ports listed at IRQ3 and IRQ4. Remember that an IRQ (interrupt request line) is necessary to inform your computer when a device needs attention. Thus, every COM port on your PC needs an IRQ line in order to draw attention to itself. If it doesn't have one, it can't communicate with the computer.

But what of COM3 and COM4? There is no IRQ listed for them in this table. Exactly! In an interesting move, the designers for the ISA bus (used in the IBM PC/AT) decided to save a few IRQs by making IRQ4 work for both COM1 and COM3, and IRQ3 work for both COM2 and COM4. Violà! Instant confusion. If you have your mouse plugged into COM1 and a modem in COM3, neither one can communicate effectively with the computer. When the computer receives an interrupt, it doesn't know which device to pay attention to.

You should pick which COM port you want to use by keeping in mind the uses to which you are putting the other ports. Once you decide on one, it is pretty easy to set the modem up. Typically they use switches to allow you to set this sort of configuration information, regardless of whether the modem is internal or external.

Switches on the back of an internal modem.

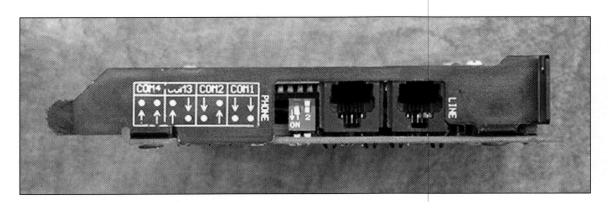

TROUBLESHOOTING COMMUNICATIONS PROBLEMS

As you have discovered, the biggest source of modem problems is IRQ conflicts. You also can run into problems with noisy phone lines, bad cable connections, and call waiting. That's right, an incoming call with call waiting will often disconnect any current modem communication.

PROBLEM: I installed my modem, and everything seemed to be fine. But now I can't get my communications software to work with it. Why?

- The first place to look is in the communications software manual. Different communications packages have different settings that you need to configure to make them work. Make sure that the software is using the COM port to which the modem is connected.

PROBLEM: My modem stopped talking to me. Is it mad?

- Probably not. In most instances, this is a case of an unplugged wire or, in the case of an internal modem, incorrect COM port settings. Check your settings and connections, and try again.

PROBLEM: When I use my communications software to connect with another system, all I see on-screen is garbage. Why?

- Many variables have to be just right for meaningful communication to occur between two computers. This symptom is typical for a system in which your communication parameters do not match those used by the remote system. Review the remote system information to see if you can determine the parameters that should be used. You are particularly interested in the number of data bits, stop bits, the parity setting, and the connection speed (in bps). Make sure your system uses these same settings, and try again.

  It's also possible that you're plagued by noise on your telephone line. Line noise will corrupt the data bits leaving and entering your modem, resulting in garbage on-screen.

PROBLEM: My modem won't hang up! How do I get off the phone?

- Press Ctrl+H or Ctrl+X. If this doesn't work, try exiting your communications software. If you're still stuck on the line, you may have to reboot to disconnect. If this happens, review your software configuration to confirm that your modem settings are correct.

PROBLEM: My modem causes my mouse to act funny (or vice versa). What's up?

- This is most definitely a COM port conflict. You probably have your mouse on COM1 and your modem on COM3 (or one is on COM2 and the other on COM4). You need to change the COM port assignment for one of the devices to an adjacent port.

CHOOSING A MODEM

Modems are available today with a wide range of capabilities, in a vast number of configurations. Perhaps the first decision you need to make is whether you want an internal or an external modem. An internal modem plugs into a slot in your computer like any other adapter card.

An example of an internal modem.

An example of an external modem.

You also can get an external modem, which many people like because it does not require a computer slot, and they can use it among several different computers.

External modems don't have to be this large. There are external modems on the market that are smaller than your checkbook. These are particularly well-suited for use with portable computers.

Besides the physical configuration of the modem, there are only a few items of importance when you are looking for a modem. These are speed, error correction, and data compression. Each of these topics is discussed in the following sections.

The speed of a modem is best measured in bps (bits per second). The bps rate tells you how many bits (individual pieces) of data the modem can send per second. Since each computer character is made up of eight bits, knowing the bps makes it easy to tell how fast a modem can send information.

> **NOTE:** Another commonly used measurement of modem speed is baud rate. The baud rate measures the number of times per second a modem can modulate (change the amplitude or frequency) its signal. If a modem can modulate its signal 9,600 times per second, it is considered to run at 9,600 baud. Baud rates are not as accurate a performance measurement as bits per second, because a particular baud may carry multiple bits—modems that carry eight bits per baud move data faster than modems that carry only four bits per baud.

In practical terms, the faster a modem is, the better it is—and the more expensive it is. Actually, it is not a lot more expensive. While you can still find 2,400 bps modems for under $100, you also can find 14,400 bps modems for under $200.

One of the things that may temper this discussion is that you must have modems on both ends of a link that can communicate at the same speeds. Thus, if you want to communicate with someone else at 9,600 bps, both of your systems must have modems that can operate at this speed. The good news is that most modems that can attain the higher speeds also can "step down" to the lower speeds. Thus, you can use a 14,400 bps modem to communicate at slower speeds such as 9,600, 2,400, or even 300 bps.

Lately, modems have been incorporating standard error correction protocols in their internal programs. These protocols are procedures for how errors should be recognized and corrected. The only error correction protocol you should pay attention to is called V.42; if your modem has it, that's good.

EXAMPLE

FAX modems combine a FAX machine and a modem into a single computer device. This means you not only can send and receive data to and from other computers, but you also can send and receive faxes.

FAX modems are great for sending information without the need to leave your office. They also are great if you have a PC at home and you don't want to purchase a separate FAX machine.

Installing an Internal Modem

Installing a modem allows you to tap into the many sources of information, education, debate, and entertainment that make up the "information super-highway." Follow these steps to install an internal modem in your computer:

1 Begin by locating the proper slot for your modem card.

Removing the slot cover for the internal modem.

2 If there is a slot cover at the rear of the computer case, where the external part of the adapter card will be situated, remove the cover.

Sliding the internal modem into its slot.

3 Slide the modem card straight down into the slot. The rear of the adapter card should slide into the slot at the rear of the computer case, and the edge connector should fit firmly in the slot on the motherboard. You may need to apply a bit of downward pressure to firmly seat the adapter card.

4 Once the modem is fully seated within the adapter card slot, replace the retaining screw so it secures the adapter card in place.

5 Now connect the modem to a phone line. The next section explains how to do this.

Fastening the retaining screw.

INSTALLING AN EXTERNAL MODEM

If you are installing an external modem, all you need to do is use a serial cable to connect the modem to a serial port on your computer. Sometimes, the proper cable is supplied with the modem; many times it is not. You should check before you leave the store to make sure you have a cable that will work. In selecting a cable, you should keep the following points in mind:

- Make sure the cable has the proper connectors. You will need either a 9-pin to 25-pin cable or a 25-pin to 25-pin cable, depending on what your COM port looks like on the back of your computer. Figure 8.6 shows what these connections on your PC generally look like.

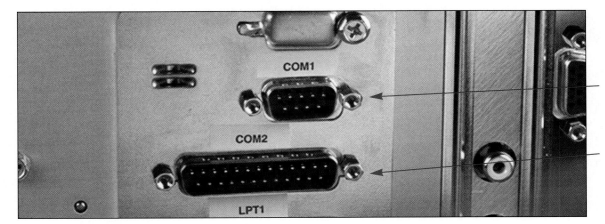

Connections on the back of your PC.

A 9-pin serial port.

A 25-pin serial port.

- Regardless of the cable you get, it should use female-to-male connectors.

- Make sure the cable is designed specifically for modems. Sometimes these are referred to as null-modem cables.

- Make sure the cable is long enough to reach from your PC to where you will place your modem.

HOOKING UP THE PHONE LINE

Now you can plug in your phone line. Every modem vendor supplies a phone cord with its modems, but you can use any phone cord that you would normally use to connect your phone to the wall outlet. This cord should have RJ-11 connectors.

The connector on the end of a phone line.

An RJ-11 plug.

On the back of your modem (internal or external) is a jack into which this cord is plugged. The jack is typically labeled *line* or *wall*. Some new modems do not have labels on their RJ-11 jacks. This is because either jack can be used for the wall outlet or for a phone. The modem automatically detects which is which.

Connections on the back of an external modem.

Power switch.

Power connector.

Used to connect the modem to your PC.

Connect this to a wall phone outlet.

Connect this to a telephone.

Notice that most modems have two RJ-11 connectors on the back. You already know that one of these is connected by a cable to the phone jack on your wall. The other is used to run a line to a telephone. If the modem is not in use, the phone signal passes straight through the modem, allowing you to use the line. If the modem is in use, the telephone is disabled so that you can't interfere with the data connection.

TESTING YOUR MODEM

Once your modem is hooked up properly, you will need to test it. Some modems come with testing software. If yours does not, you will need to use some sort of communications software to do the test.

> **NOTE:** After you install your modem, you need to configure your communications software so that it knows how to communicate with your modem. This involves informing the software to which serial port your modem is attached and the speed your modem communicates. Refer to your software documentation for more information.

Once your communications software is installed, follow these steps:

- Start the communications software.

- Enter terminal mode, if necessary.

- Enter the following command, and then press Enter.

  `atdt`

You should hear a dial tone and see a response such as OK appear on-screen. You now know that your PC is connected properly with your modem. If it does not work, either your communications software is installed incorrectly or you do not have the modem installed properly.

CHAPTER 15
Keyboards and Mice

UNDERSTANDING INPUT DEVICES

On most computer systems there are two ways to input information—the keyboard or the mouse.

A mouse is a pointing device used to point at and select items on-screen. There are other kinds of pointing devices, including joysticks, trackballs, light pens, touch screens, and graphics tablets, but we'll focus on the mouse for now.

Recognizing the importance of the mouse to computing, it is reasonable to look at either adding a mouse to your system or upgrading the mouse you have. Why would you want to upgrade your current mouse? Primarily because many systems come with a mouse that most people would consider less than optimal.

A typical mouse for use with a PC.

This cable connects with the PC.

This mouse has two buttons.

This is the mouse.

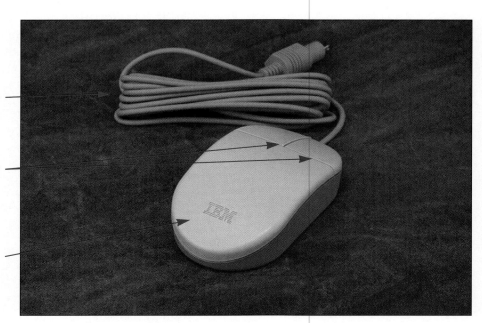

Most mice consist of nothing more than a plastic shell with two or three buttons built into it. Out of one end of the mouse is a cord that connects with your PC. This cord is used to send information to the PC about movement and button clicks.

If you turn the mouse over, on the bottom is a small ball that rolls as you move the mouse across a surface. This provides the movement information that the mouse needs in order to operate. The best roller balls are made of a textured rubber that provides a bit of friction as the mouse moves.

Looking at the bottom of a mouse.

The roller ball.

A keyboard is basically just a bunch of switches that send electrical impulses to the system unit when you press a key. In fact, some of the original computer keyboards didn't even have keys; they had flat touch pads. Touch typists didn't like these "Chiclet" keyboards, however, so mechanical devices were added to give a better feel to the typing action.

The enhanced keyboard.

A really enhanced keyboard.

There are two major types of keyboards available on personal computers today, the *regular keyboard* and the *enhanced keyboard*. The enhanced keyboard has a few more keys than the regular keyboard and is sold with most PCs marketed today. It is possible, in some cases, to replace a regular keyboard with an enhanced keyboard.

NOTE: Some manufacturers, such as Gateway and Northgate, make keyboards that combine the left-hand function keys of the regular keyboard with the extra keys and top-mounted function keys of the enhanced keyboard.

CONNECTING A MOUSE

A mouse can be connected to your system in any of three ways: a serial port, a bus connection, or a mouse port.

A serial port is the most common method of connecting a mouse. One end of the mouse cord has a serial connector on it that you simply plug into an available serial port on the back of your PC.

The serial connector on the end of the mouse cord.

Although it is probably the least used method of connecting a mouse, you can use what is referred to as a bus connection. This means that you add an adapter board to your PC that does nothing but control the mouse. Most people shy away from this because it takes up a valuable slot in your PC. You may want to use this approach, however, if your serial ports are already connected to other devices.

Many PCs these days are coming equipped with a dedicated mouse port. This is similar to the bus approach, except that the circuitry is built directly into the PC's motherboard. There is no need to take up a slot with a bus card, nor is there a need to occupy a serial port. For example, the IBM PS/Valuepoint computer includes a mouse port connector.

The mouse port connector on an IBM PS/Valuepoint.

The mouse port.

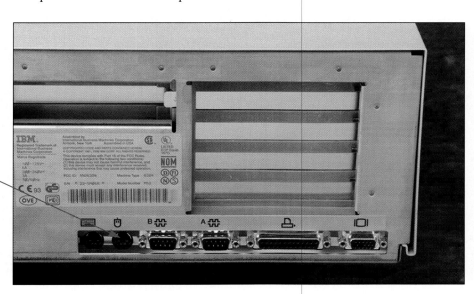

Notice that the mouse port connector does not use the same type of connector as was used earlier for the serial mouse. To remedy this, many mouse manufacturers provide an adapter that allows you to connect the serial mouse to a mouse port.

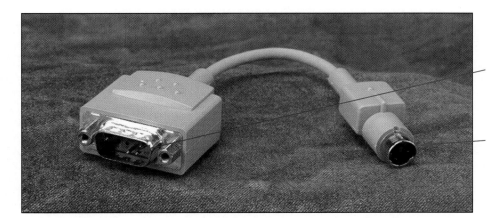

A mouse port adapter.

The serial connector is plugged in here.

This plug is connected to the mouse port on the PC.

A mouse can't work without software drivers. What drivers should you use? Quite honestly, you should use those supplied with your mouse. Many mice on the market are designed to emulate the Microsoft Mouse; in this instance, you can use the Microsoft Mouse driver. This driver is typically provided with new versions of DOS or with Windows. If your mouse is not compatible with the Microsoft Mouse, you will need to use a different driver.

If you want the mouse to be available to all programs, it is best to install the driver either through your CONFIG.SYS or AUTOEXEC.BAT files. For example, the following command line, added to your CONFIG.SYS file, loads the device driver for the Microsoft Mouse:

```
device = c:\mouse\mouse.sys
```

Similarly, the following line loads the device driver from within the AUTOEXEC.BAT file:

```
c:\mouse\mouse.com
```

Notice that one method uses the file MOUSE.SYS and the other method uses the file MOUSE.COM. The method you use is up to you, but the vendor supplying the device driver may require a certain technique. (Not all vendors may provide both a COM and SYS file as Microsoft does.) There also are command-line switches you can add to either of these lines that will alter the way the mouse works. Many of these switches are specific to particular mouse vendors; you will want to review your mouse documentation for more information.

CONNECTING A KEYBOARD

All IBM-compatible PCs have a special port on the back panel specifically to connect a keyboard. Changing keyboards is as simple as unplugging the old one and connecting the new one to the keyboard port. You may need to reboot your computer to recognize the new keyboard.

The keyboard port.

Notice that some older PCs won't accept newer enhanced keyboards. In some cases the plug won't fit; in others, the plug fits but the computer won't recognize the new keyboard. If this happens, you will need to replace the keyboard with a model like the original.

TROUBLESHOOTING INPUT PROBLEMS

Most input problems come from bad connections, incorrectly installed drivers, or just plain bad hardware. When you have problems with either your mouse or keyboard, remember to check all your cables before proceeding.

Problem: I just plugged my mouse into my system and it doesn't seem to work. Why not?

- Check the cable connections to make certain the mouse cable is firmly seated in its port. Some mice, called "bus mice," have their own adapter card and use a round connector instead of the more common "D" shaped connector.

Problem: When I boot my system, I notice a message that says that the mouse was not found. I know it's here; I can see it sitting on the desk. What's wrong?

- For some reason the mouse driver can't find your mouse. The Microsoft Mouse drivers automatically detect the presence of a mouse, if they can find one. If not, you will see this message. Try checking to see if your mouse is plugged in fully. If it is, and it still won't work, plug the mouse into your other serial port. If it works then, you know that there was something on the other port that conflicted with the mouse, that the other port is configured incorrectly, or that the port just doesn't work.

Problem: The mouse works great in some software programs, but not in others. Why?

- Many software programs require that you configure them or reinstall them so they can take advantage of a mouse. Consult the documentation for the offending program to see if you can determine the steps necessary to make the program work with your mouse.

Problem: My mouse has been working for some time now, but all of a sudden it stopped. Could it have died?

- It may have, but it is more likely that the mouse's cable connector has come loose at the back of your PC. Check the connection, reboot your machine, and see if the mouse works. If not, you may want to try another mouse (one from someone else's system which you know works on their system) at your PC to see if it will work. If the newer mouse still won't work, you should try plugging it into another serial port on your PC. It is possible (but unlikely) that your serial port has died, and not the mouse.

Problem: My keyboard won't type. What causes this?

- First, make sure the keyboard is firmly connected to your computer. Now reboot your computer. If this doesn't solve your problem, you probably have a bad keyboard. See if connecting a new keyboard to your system fixes the problem.

CHAPTER 16
Joysticks and Game Ports

UNDERSTANDING PC GAME EQUIPMENT

The many action and simulation games that have hit the market have created a huge demand for peripherals that enhance their play value on a normal PC. Although you can use the keyboard or a mouse, joysticks make the games much easier to use and increase the realism, particularly for flight simulation software and shoot-'em-up games.

Joysticks are used primarily for entertainment software, not for general business applications (except possibly for disabled users). By using one, you can get a more realistic feel for buzzing the Sears Tower with your flight simulator, or for zapping evil aliens in the latest space weapons battle.

Not surprisingly, joysticks simulate a control device used in airplanes. They are nothing but an upright handle you can tilt in any direction. The information transmitted to the PC is based on the direction of the movement and how hard and fast you move in that direction. Most joysticks also include one or two control buttons.

A typical joystick.

The control buttons.

The joystick handle.

The cable for connecting to the PC.

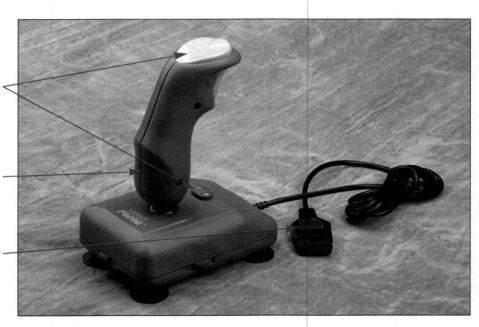

Believe it or not, there are even more models of joysticks on the market than there are mice. This is because the "feel" of a joystick is even more subjective than that of a mouse.

> **NOTE:** If you are going to purchase a joystick, plan on spending a bit of time at your computer dealer picking out the one that feels best to you. Once you make a decision, you may want to keep your receipt so that you can return it if it doesn't feel right after you start using it with your favorite software program.

Joysticks don't connect through normal COM ports like mice; you have to connect your joystick to your computer through a special game port connector. These connectors are typically contained on multi-function I/O cards or on sound cards. If you do not have those, you can purchase a special game I/O card at many full-service computer stores. These cards are extremely inexpensive, many selling for under $15. One of the advantages to these game I/O cards is that some of them offer the ability to connect two joysticks at the same time. This is great, provided you have software that can recognize and accept input from both joysticks.

CONNECTING A GAME PORT

Here is how to add a game port to your computer:

1 To install a game port in your PC, locate an open slot on your motherboard.

Removing a slot cover.

2 If there is a slot cover at the rear of the computer case (where the external part of the adapter card will be situated), remove the cover.

Sliding a game port into its slot.

3 Slide the game card straight down into the slot. The rear of the card should slide into the slot at the rear of the computer case, and the edge connector should seat firmly in the slot on the motherboard. You may need to apply a bit of downward pressure to firmly seat the card.

Fastening the retaining screw.

4 Once the game port is fully seated within the adapter card slot, replace the retaining screw so that it secures the adapter card in place.

5 Now you can connect your joystick to the back of the game port and merrily zap your life away!

CONNECTING A JOYSTICK

To connect a joystick, simply plug the cable running from the joystick into the game port. Unlike the mouse, there are no software drivers to install; the routines to access the game port are built directly into your BIOS chips (and have been since July 1986). You may, however, need to inform your software that the joystick is installed; you also may need to calibrate the joystick so that it works correctly with that software. This is all handled by the specific software (refer to your program documentation for more information).

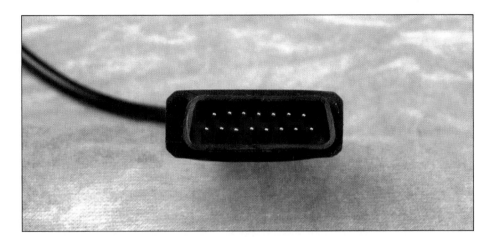

A joystick connector.

NOTE: If the joystick fails to work, there are two probable causes to check. First, you may have a conflict between the game port and another I/O port on your PC—refer to Chapter 5, "System Ports," to learn more about possible conflicts. Another possibility is that your game software isn't expecting to use a joystick. Confirm that you have configured your software to use a joystick.

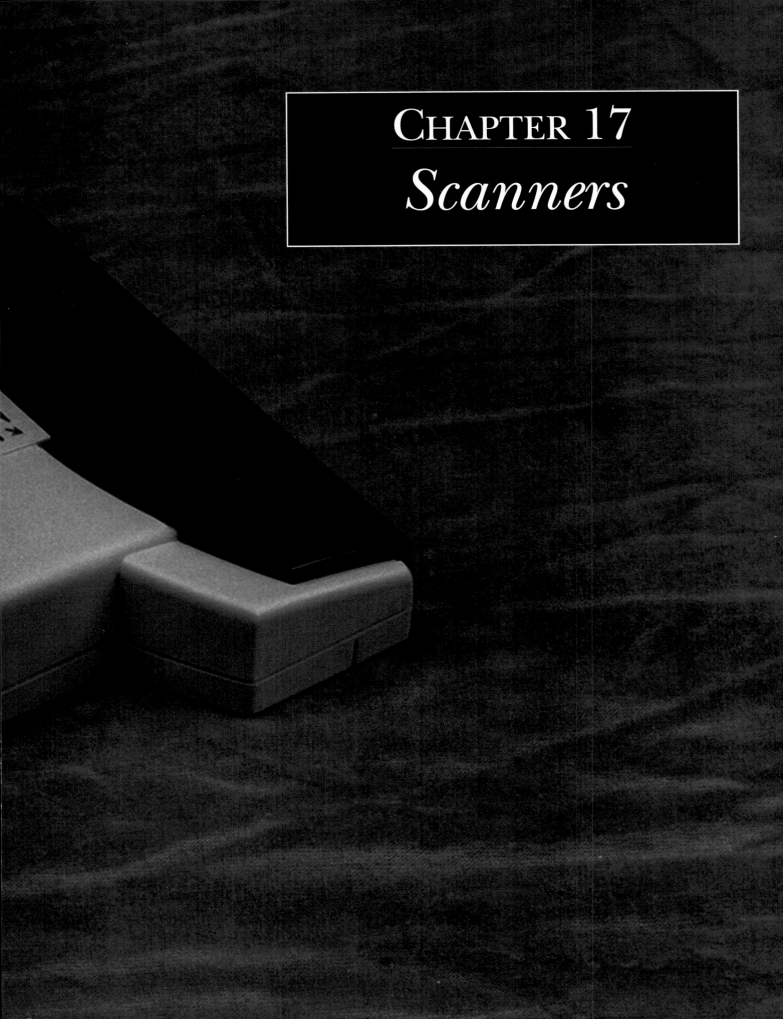

CHAPTER 17
Scanners

UNDERSTANDING SCANNERS

Computer scanners work in a manner similar to photocopiers. Both computer scanners and photocopiers move a bright light across the page and measure the amount of light being reflected. Since different colors (or shades of gray) reflect different amounts of light, the scanning process is able to construct a duplicate of the image being scanned from the reflections. The photocopier copies this duplicate image onto another page; the scanner uses the computer to create a digital duplicate of the page being scanned.

Scanners come in several different styles. The two most popular are flat-bed scanners and hand-held scanners. Flat-bed scanners look like small photocopiers. Hand-held scanners look like a "T" with a cable attached.

A Logitech ScanMan 256 gray scale scanner.

This end of the scanner holds the light bar that shines on the page.

This end holds the electronics that measure the amount of reflected light.

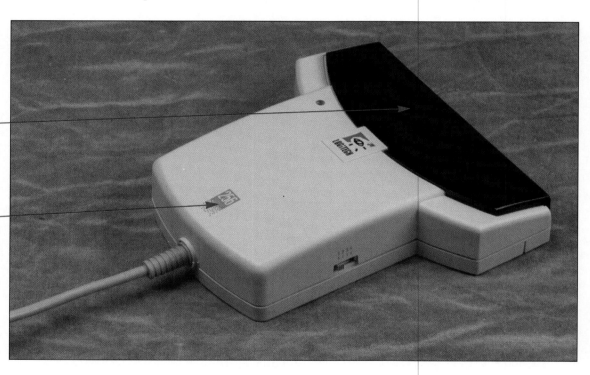

Images captured with a scanner are basically a collection of closely spaced dots, or bits, of data. The computer maps these bits of data into the shape of the scanned image. Not surprisingly, the resulting images are called "bitmaps."

A scanner's resolution is measured in terms of the number of dots per inch (dpi) it is capable of mapping. The more dots that are mapped per inch, the more accurate the image.

Scanners work in color, gray scale, or black and white. The color scanners are the most complex and the most expensive, followed by gray scale scanners, and simple black-and-white scanners.

- **Color Scanners** process the light reflected from the image through red, green and blue filters. By layering these three images together, a full color image can be stored digitally. Typical PC compatible color scanners cost as little as $500, or as much as $2,500.

- **Gray Scale Scanners** map the various colors to shades of gray, producing images in shades of gray instead of just black and white. Gray scale scanners usually cost about $225 for handheld models and up to $2,000 for desktop models.

- **Black and White Scanners** don't differentiate between different colors, or varying shades of gray. As the image is scanned, the computer maps the image to either white (no image at all) or black (all other colors).

> **NOTE:** Black and white printers can approximate shades of gray by fooling the human eye. They do this by spacing the black dots at different densities. If you place black dots close together into a square pattern, the pattern will appear black. If you place them farther apart, the square will look gray to the human eye—our eye tries to "fill" the space between the dots and "mixes" the white space with the black dots.

INSTALLING A HAND SCANNER

Here is how to add a Logitech hand scanner to your computer:

1 To install a scanner interface card in your PC, locate an open slot on your motherboard.

Removing a slot cover.

2 Remove the slot cover at the rear of the computer case where the external part of the adapter card will be situated.

Aligning a scan-
ner interface card.

Make certain the
card is positioned
over the slot.

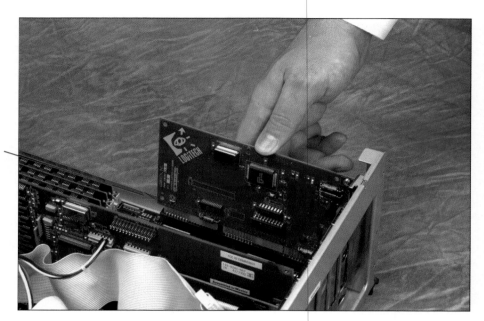

3 Align the adapter card over the slot.

After aligning the
card, use two
hands to press it
firmly into the slot.

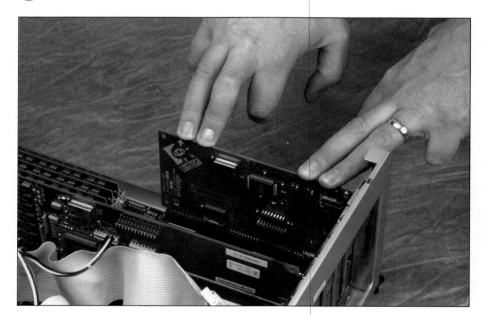

4 Slide the adapter straight down into the slot. The rear of the card
should slide into the slot at the rear of the computer case, and the edge
connector should seat firmly in the slot on the motherboard. You may
need to apply a bit of downward pressure to firmly seat the card.

5 Once the scanner interface card is fully seated within the adapter card
slot, replace the retaining screw so it secures the adapter card in place.

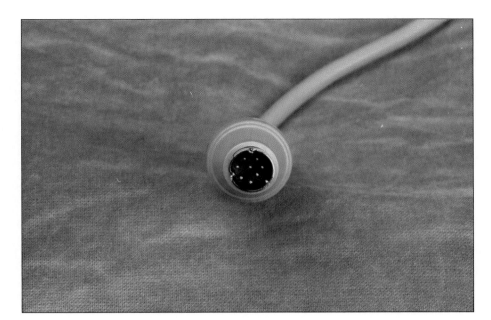

Plug the scanner's cable . . .

. . . into this port.

6 Connect the end of the scanner's cable to the port in the back of the scanner's adapter card.

Now you're ready to reassemble your computer, install the scanning software, and give it a test run.

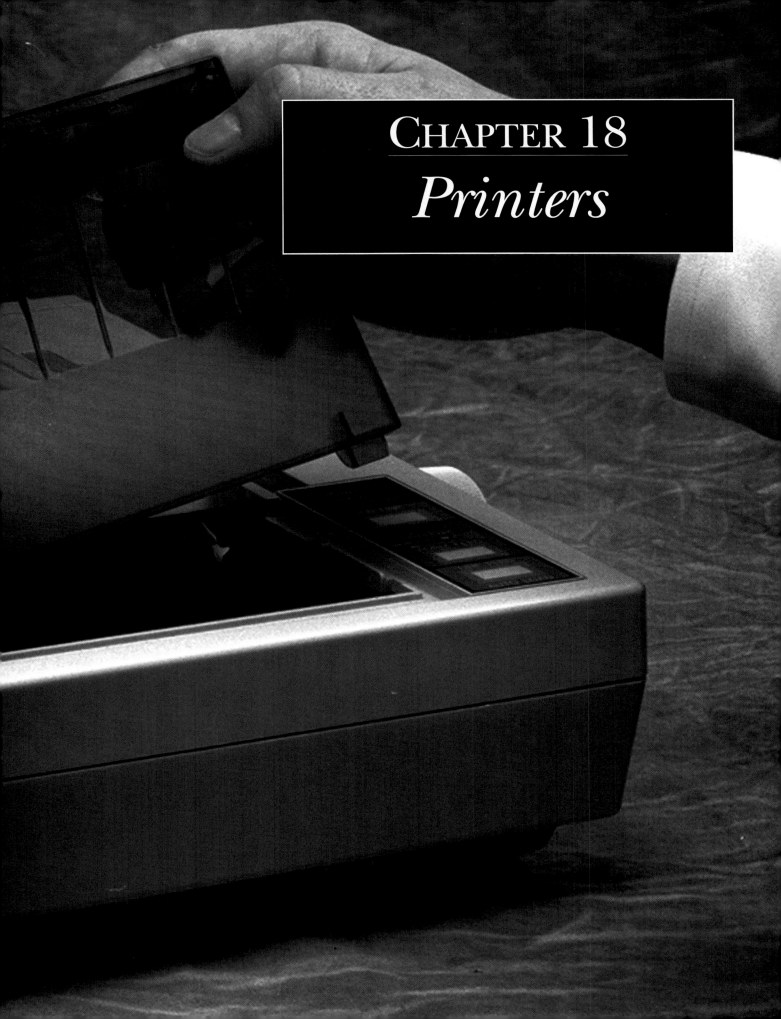

CHAPTER 18
Printers

UNDERSTANDING PRINTERS

Printers tend to be one of the most complex devices attached to your computer. They also are one of the most abused, neglected, and overlooked peripherals. We always seem to take them for granted, day after day, until one day they stop working. Those are the times when we typically start considering getting a new printer.

In the PC world, there are two broad categories of printers: black-and-white or color. There are three big differences between printers in these categories:

- What they print

- How they print

- What they cost

The first difference should be obvious—one type prints in color, and the other in black-and-white. The second may not be quite as obvious, unless, of course, you like poking around inside printers. Printing mechanisms in black-and-white printers tend to be rather simple. Those that print in color, on the other hand, need much more complex mechanisms to put three, four, or however many colors on a piece of paper.

Finally, black-and-white printers, regardless of their type, are quite a bit less expensive than color printers. In many instances, a color counterpart to a black-and-white printer may cost anywhere from two to three times as much money.

Within each printer category, there is a further breakdown into types. While there are many, many different types of printers on the market, the majority of them fall into one of three categories:

- Dot-matrix

- Inkjet

- Laser

Dot-matrix printers use a print head composed of a series of vertically-aligned pins that strike the paper as the print head moves from left to right. These pins produce a series of dots, and each character is an array of dots.

Of course, dot-matrix printers have enough pins that the dots typically overlap a bit, thereby giving the illusion of complete lines. The two most common types of dot-matrix printers use print heads that contain either nine or 24 pins. The greater the number of pins, the more overlap there is and the higher quality the printing.

In some ways, inkjet printers are similar to dot-matrix printers. The difference is in how ink is placed on the paper. Where a dot-matrix printer strikes a ribbon that leaves an impression, an inkjet printer squirts ink through a series of small nozzles to create images. These nozzles, or jets, are arranged vertically in a moving print head (as are the pins in a dot-matrix printer). As the print head moves across the page, the jets turn on and off, squirting ink at just the right time in order to literally paint an image on the paper.

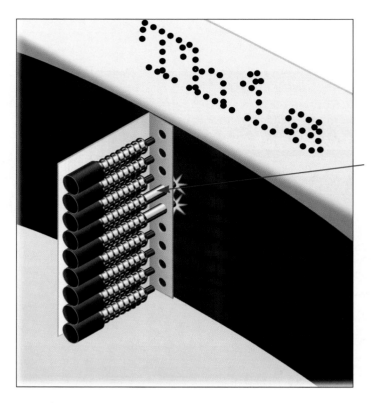

An example of how a dot-matrix printer creates characters.

Dot-matrix printers hammer metal pins into an ink-coated ribbon and against the paper.

An example of a laser printer.

The final printer type, laser printers, function in a manner similar to office copiers. Instead of the image coming from a camera lens taking a picture of an original, the image is composed from the data sent from your PC.

These printers even look like small office copiers. That's because they use essentially the same internal mechanisms to put ink on paper. As the paper moves through the machine, toner is deposited in the patterns needed. The paper then travels through a fuser, which applies heat to bond the toner to the paper.

CHOOSING A PRINTER

When you want to purchase a printer, there are several factors you need to weigh to make the proper buying decision. The primary factor, for many people, is the budget. Printers can cost anywhere from a couple of hundred dollars (for low-price dot-matrix printers) to almost $100,000 (for high-speed, high-capacity laser printers). Somewhere in the middle is the printer you want.

What items affect price? The answer varies based on printer type, but in general, the following factors determine how much the vendor charges:

- **Print quality.** Printers with more print head pins or a greater resolution (for laser and inkjet printers) cost more and give the best-looking output.

- **Print speed.** The speed at which the printer places images on the paper is a big consideration. Fast printers cost more than slow ones.

- **Print mechanism.** Dot-matrix and inkjet printers cost less than laser. (It's that simple.)

- **Paper handling.** Printers that offer fancy handling options such as single sheet, collating, envelopes, or large-capacity paper bins cost more than those with simple features.

- **Vendor name.** Vendors do tend to play off their name, so you will pay more for a Hewlett Packard, Okidata, or Epson than you will for brands with lesser-known names.

Printers can be configured with a variety of different interfaces that allow you to connect them as you desire. Most personal printers use a parallel or serial interface. These printers are easy to connect and use right away. Take a look at the back of a printer, and you can generally tell right away whether it uses a parallel or serial interface. Parallel printers have a female Centronics parallel connector.

Most dot-matrix or inkjet printers will have this type of parallel connection. Other printers may have strictly a serial connection, which is a female 25-pin connector. If you have a laser printer, however, there is a good chance it has both types of connections—serial and parallel.

A Centronics parallel connector on a printer.

Cable connections on the back of a laser printer.

For connecting to a parallel port.

For connecting to a serial port.

Other printers, particularly those that are higher-priced or that are intended to be used by more than one person, may include different types of interfaces. Some of the higher-quality laser printers, such as those from Hewlett-Packard or QMS, come configured with network adapters so they plug right into a network and serve as a print station for an entire department.

UNHOOKING YOUR OLD PRINTER

If you get a new printer, the first thing you need to do is to remove your old printer. This simple process can be boiled down to the following steps:

Removing paper from the printer.

1 Remove the paper from the printer.

2 Turn off the printer (there is no need to turn off your PC).

Disconnecting the cable from the printer.

Tip: *It is a good idea to keep your old printer close at hand until you are sure your new printer is working correctly.*

3 Disconnect the cable from the rear of the printer.

4 Unplug the printer's power cord from the wall.

5 Move the printer out of the way.

ADDING A NEW PRINTER

Adding a new printer is one of the easier upgrades to your system—you don't need to disassemble your computer and there are seldom any switches to set. Here is how to add a new printer to your system:

1 The first step in adding a new printer is to unpack it from its shipping container. Make sure you remove any shipping materials that may have been placed inside the printer. For example, it is not unusual for dot-matrix printers to have some sort of shipping material that stops the print head from moving during transit. Forgetting to remove these items prior to using the printer can result in damage to the printer.

Hooking up the printer cable to your PC.

2 Connect the printer to your PC. Make sure you have the proper cable on hand in order to make the connection. If your printer has a parallel interface, you need a parallel cable. Likewise, if it is a serial printer, you need a serial cable.

3 Plug the printer's power cord into the wall. Some printers may have a detachable power cord, so make sure it is installed correctly in the power receptacle at the back of the printer, as well as plugged into the wall.

4 Now you can add to the printer whatever it is that makes marks on your paper. In a dot-matrix printer, this is the ribbon; in an inkjet printer it is the ink cartridge; and in a laser printer it is the toner cartridge.

REPLACING PRINTER RIBBONS (DOT-MATRIX PRINTERS)

CAUTION: Moving the print head while the printer is still turned on can damage the printer and may cause injury. That darn old print head can move pretty fast. Make sure the power is off before moving the print head.

Believe it or not, adding a ribbon to a dot-matrix printer is perhaps the most difficult to describe of all these processes. This is because there are so many different printer ribbons that are all added in different ways. In general, however, you should do the following:

1 Make sure the printer is turned off.

Moving the print head to the center of the printer.

2 Slide the print head to the center of the printer.

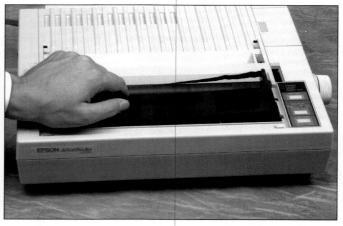

Removing the old ribbon.

3 Remove the old ribbon, if one was previously installed. Release the retaining clips on both sides of the ribbon, and then lift it out of the printer.

The ribbon goes between the print head and the ink sheild.

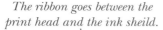

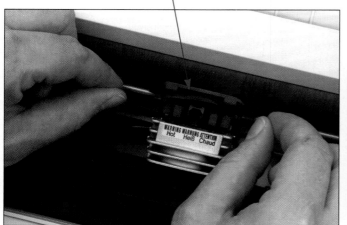

Properly threading the ribbon.

4 Insert the new ribbon, making sure the ribbon is between the print head and the paper.

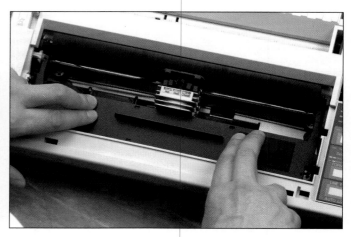

Snapping the ribbon cartridge in place.

5 Make sure the ribbon is firmly seated in its carrier, with any retaining clips in place.

6 Turn on the printer.

REPLACING AN INK CARTRIDGE (INKJET PRINTERS)

Adding an ink cartridge to an inkjet printer is similar in nature to adding a ribbon to a dot-matrix printer. You do, however, need to do a bit more prep work on the ink cartridge. Here is how to change a print cartridge in a Hewlett-Packard DeskJet printer (most other inkjet printers are very similar):

1 Remove the cartridge from its packaging, and then remove the seal that covers the side facing the paper. Don't touch the copper colored portions of the cartridge; oil from your fingers can damage the printing mechanism.

Pull top of cartridge toward thumb to release.

Place new cartridge in holder and press toward green dot.

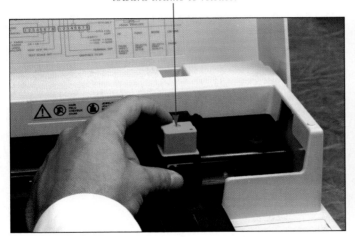

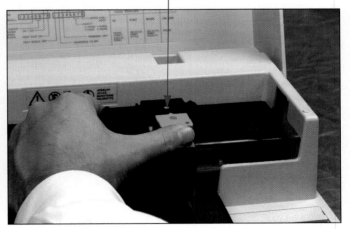

Removing the old ink cartridge.

The new ink cartridge in place.

2 If you need to remove an old ink cartridge, gently press the top of the cartridge backwards, away from the green dot, to snap the cartridge loose.

3 Slide the new cartridge into the printer. Make sure the cartridge is oriented properly—the pointed notch on the ink cartridge points toward the green dot on the cartridge holder.

REPLACING A TONER CARTRIDGE (LASER PRINTERS)

Adding a toner cartridge to a laser printer is very easy. To do so, follow these steps:

1 Open the front or top of the laser printer. (The way you open it varies depending on the model. You may want to check your documentation the first time you do this.)

Pull green tab.

The toner cartridge.

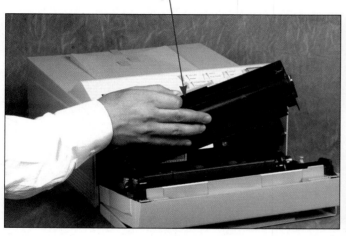

Removing a toner cartridge from a laser printer.

Inserting a toner cartridge in a laser printer.

2 If there is currently a toner cartridge in the printer, remove it by pulling up and out.

3 Take the new toner cartridge out of its packaging and hold it with one hand on each end of the cartridge. Since some of the toner may have shifted or settled during shipment, gently rock the toner cartridge to distribute the toner evenly.

4 Remove any seal that may have been put in place on the cartridge. Different toner cartridges have different types of seals, so check the instructions that came with the cartridge to see where the seal is and how it is removed.

5 Finally, slide the cartridge into the laser printer. It should fit fully within the printer. When it has been inserted, close the front or top of the printer.

TROUBLESHOOTING PRINTER PROBLEMS

Because the printer is a mechanical device, it's prone to mechanical problems. Remember to check and clean all moving parts periodically.

PROBLEM: Why are all my printouts garbled?

- The most common cause of this is a disconnected (or poorly connected) printer cable. You also may have the wrong printer driver selected in your software program.

PROBLEM: My paper always seems to bunch up under the tractor feed. Why is this?

- Usually this is a result of three conditions. The first possibility is that the paper is not threaded through the tractors correctly (one side is further in than the other, making the paper crooked). Another is that the paper does not have the right horizontal tension on it. Check to make sure that the paper is not too taut and not too loose between the tractors. The other possibility is that the paper is too thick for the printer.

PROBLEM: My printouts are starting to get pretty light.

- You probably need to change the ribbon or toner cartridge. Make a change and see if that fixes the problem. Another option (for a dot-matrix printer) is to check the paper thickness lever.

PROBLEM: There are vertical streaks running through the pages I just printed on my laser printer. What would cause that?

- Typically, it is the result of a defective toner cartridge. Change the toner cartridge and try again.

PROBLEM: The printout from my laser printer is way too dark. Can it be toned down?

- Most laser printers include some sort of control knob that allows you to change the print density of whatever is printed. Check your laser printer manual for details.

PROBLEM: The paper in my laser printer (or inkjet printer) keeps jamming. Why is that?

- This may be due to two things. First, you may be trying to use a paper that is too thick for your printer. Check your manual to see if your paper is outside of what your printer will accept.

  The second reason could be "paper curl." If you use regular photocopy paper in your printer, look at the end of the paper ream. Notice that there is information on which way the paper should be fed into the printer (or copier).

KM44C256AP-10
915 KOREA
KM44C256AP-10
915 KOREA
KM44C256AP-10
915 KOREA
KM44C256AP-10
915 KOREA
KM44C256AP-10
915 KOREA
KM44C256AP-10
914 KOREA
KM44C256AP-10
915 KOREA
KM44C256AP-10
915 KOREA
KM44C256AP-10
915 KOREA
KM44C256AP-10
915 KOREA
KM44C256AP-10
915 KOREA
KM44C256AP-10
917 KOREA
KM44C256AP-10
915 KOREA
KM44C256AP-10
915 KOREA
KM44C256AP-10
915 KOREA
KM44C256AP-10
914 KOREA
NEC JAPAN
D41256C -10
8851AU009
NEC JAPAN
D41256C -10
8851AU009
NEC JAPAN
D41256C -10
8851AU009
NEC JAPAN
D41256C -10
8851AU009
NEC JAPAN
D41256C -10
8851AU009

Glossary

KM44C256AP-10
915 KOREA
KM44C256AP-10
915 KOREA
KM44C256AP-10
915 KOREA
KM44C256AP-10
915 KOREA
KM44C256AP-10
914 KOREA
KM44C256AP-10
915 KOREA
KM44C256AP-10
915 KOREA
KM44C256AP-10
915 KOREA
KM44C256AP-10
915 KOREA
KM44C256AP-10
917 KOREA
KM44C256AP-10
915 KOREA
KM44C256AP-10
915 KOREA
KM44C256AP-10
915 KOREA
NEC JAPAN
D41256C -10
8851AU009
NEC JAPAN
D41256C -10
8851AU009
NEC JAPAN
D41256C -10
8851AU009
NEC JAPAN
D41256C -10
8851AU009

101 key-enhanced keyboard A current standard in keyboard design for keyboards supporting a large number of different keys.

access time Average time it takes for a given hard disk to move the read/write head into position to read a requested sector.

acknowledge line A line on a parallel connection which is used to indicate when the device is ready for more data.

acoustic modem A modem which connects not to the phone line, but to the phone handset.

address A value that indicates a location in memory. Also, a value that indicates a specific device on a network.

adventure game A computer game which involves controlling a character through a series of challenges and puzzles.

amplitude The size of a wave.

analog Representing a value as an infinitely variable signal.

AND A logical operator that puts out the value of true (or 1) only if both values going in are true (or 1).

arcade game An action-oriented computer game.

archive utility A program which stores a group of files as a single, smaller file.

ASCII Abbreviation for American Standard Code for Information Interchange, a method of encoding text as binary values.

assembler A program that takes a program written in assembly language and turns it into machine language.

auto feed pin A line on a parallel I/O connection, used by the computer to tell the printer whether to automatically advance the paper with each carriage return.

AUTOEXEC.BAT A batch file program that is run by DOS at start-up.

background printing A feature which allows a file to be printed while the computer can still work on other processes.

backup A stored duplicate copy of disk information.

base 2 See *binary.*

base 16 See *hexadecimal.*

batch files Programs written as a series of commands interpreted by the operating system.

baud A measurement of how many times per second a modem can send information, sometimes also used to mean *bits per second.*

BBS See *Bulletin Board System.*

binary A way of encoding numbers as a series of bits.

binary logic A system of logic built around comparisons between two bits.

BIOS Abbreviation for Basic Input/Output System, the program that controls the basic functions of communications between the processor and the I/O devices.

bit The smallest unit of information, which represents one of two values (usually 0 and 1). Also, the memory or disk space used to hold that information.

boot block The first sector of a disk, used to store the operating system loading programs.

bps Abbreviation for bits per second, a measurement of communication speed.

buffer A storage area of memory which holds information going from one place to another, until the receiving device is ready to accept it.

Bulletin board system A computer set up to distribute messages over a modem. Abbreviated BBS.

burning ROMs Using a special device to store information in ROM chips.

busy line A communications line on a parallel connection, used to tell the computer that the device is busy with the information it already received.

byte Eight bits of information. A single byte can have 256 different values.

CAD See *computer-aided design.*

carriage A metal rod in a printer that the print head slides along.

cathode A device that shoots out electrons.

cathode ray tube The picture tube of a monitor. Abbreviated CRT.

CD-ROM Abbreviation for Compact Disk Read-Only Memory. Optically readable disks used to distribute large amounts of information.

cell A single space on a spreadsheet grid.

central processing unit The main command-interpreting chip in a computer. Abbreviated CPU.

Centronics-type connector A standard connector with 36 contacts, named after the printer manufacturer who developed it.

CGA Abbreviation for Color Graphics Adapter, a low-quality standard for video adapters.

checksum A value calculated on a set of data, and used to check the data's integrity.

chip A small flat square with silicon-based transistors used for logic or data storage; also, the casing on metal pins that contain the chip.

CISC Abbreviation for Complex Instruction Set Computing, a philosophy of processor design that focuses on creating processors that handle a wide range of powerful instructions.

clients Computers on a local area network which receive files from the file server.

clip art Existing art for use with computer art and desktop publication programs.

cluster A group of disk sectors allocatable as a unit.

coaxial cable A type of cable used in cable TV connections and some local area networks.

cold boot Starting a computer by turning it on.

command An instruction given to the computer by the user or by a program.

COMMAND.COM The program that handles the DOS user interface.

compiler A program that takes a program written in a programming language and translates it into machine language, so that the computer can understand it.

CompuServe B A file transfer protocol.

computer A device which processes information.

computer aided design The designing of physical objects using computer programs. Abbreviated CAD.

conductor A material that carries electricity well.

CONFIG.SYS A file used in DOS to inform the system of the presence of special devices and to set up communications with those devices.

cooperative multitasking A system of multitasking which requires that programs be designed to voluntarily return control to the operating system or environment at regular intervals.

corona wire A wire which dissipates static charge from a laser printer's drum, clearing it for printing the next page.

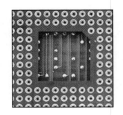

CP/M An operating system used in older computers.

CP/M—86 An early operating system for computers based around the 8086 CPU.

CPU See *central processing unit.*

cracker Someone who accesses computer systems without permission.

cradle The part of an acoustical modem in which the handset rests.

criteria A set of requirements for selecting an item from a group, as in selecting records from a database program.

CRT See *cathode ray tube.*

CTS Abbreviation for Clear To Send, the line in a serial I/O connection that the device uses to let the computer know that it is ready to receive data.

current directory The directory that your commands currently affect.

cylinder A circular portion of all of the sides in a disk.

daisywheel A disk with spokes coming out, with characters at the end of each spoke. This is part of a daisywheel printer.

daisywheel printer An impact printer which uses a daisywheel to print a fixed set of characters.

data Pieces of information.

data file A file that stores information for a program to process.

database A set of records stored as a group.

database program A program designed to maintain a set of records and generate reports based on that information.

datum A single piece of information.

DB-9 A standard connector design with 9 leads.

DB-25 A standard connector design with 25 leads.

DCD Data Carrier Detect, the line on a serial connection used to indicate that a connection has been completed.

defragmenter A program which rearranges the files so that they are in contiguous clusters.

delete To remove, as in *deleting* a file.

demodulate To decode information from modulated sound.

desktop computer A computer designed to sit on your desk.

desktop publishing program A program that lets you design the layout of printed pages.

digital Representing a value of something as one of a limited set of possible signals.

digitizing tablet An input device, on which the user draws lines, using a stylus. The lines then appear on-screen in computer art programs.

directory A grouping of files on the disk.

directory tree The organizational structure of directories on a disk.

disk A unit with one or more platters (or *discs*) which are used to store information.

disk compression utility A program which reduces the amount of space that files take up on a hard drive.

disk drive A device used to read and store information on circular media.

diskless PC A personal computer with no disk drives, designed to attach to a local area network and to use only files stored on other computers on that network.

DOS Disk Operating System, a term commonly used to refer to the operating system products MS-DOS and PC DOS.

dot pitch The spacing between the pixels on a color monitor.

dot-matrix printer An impact printer which creates images as gridworks of dots.

double-density Describes floppy disks physically capable of storing more information than regular-density disks but not as much as high-density disks.

double-spin Describes CD-ROM drives that spin the disk twice as fast as standard CD-ROM drives, so data can be read more quickly.

download To transfer files from another computer to your computer via a modem.

DPI Abbreviation for dots per inch, a measure of image resolution.

DR DOS An operating system that emulates the functions of MS-DOS.

draw program A program that lets you draw pictures made up of lines and curves.

drum The rotating cylinder at the core of a laser printer.

DSR Abbreviation for Data Set Ready, the line of a serial I/O connection that the device uses to indicate that it is on and ready.

DTR Abbreviation for Data Terminal Ready, the line of a serial I/O connection that the computer uses to indicate that it is on and ready.

e-mail See electronic mail.

EGA Abbreviation for Enhanced Graphics Adapter, a mid-quality standard for video adapters.

EISA Abbreviation for Extended Industry Standard Architecture, a standard design for system buses.

electronic mail Letters and other documents sent via networks, information services, or bulletin board systems.

electrons Negatively charged subatomic particles.

encoder wheel A wheel inside a mouse which is used to measure the speed and direction of the mouse's movement.

enhancement technology The variation of the size of dots printed by laser printers, to create sharper images.

EtherNet A set of cabling and protocol standards for local area networks.

even parity One of two methods of calculating a parity bit value.

excited Used to describe phosphorous that has been exposed to electrons.

executive word processor A word processing program with a limited but easy-to-use set of abilities.

expanded memory A system of flipping different 16-kilobyte chunks of memory into and out of the 640K addressing space to which DOS is limited.

extended-density Describes floppy disks which can store more than high-density disks.

extended memory RAM memory beyond the first megabyte.

external modem A modem which sits outside of the computer, attached via a serial port.

FAT The file allocation table, which is used to keep track of which clusters on a disk are used and which are available.

fault line A line on a parallel I/O connection used by the device to tell the computer when something has gone wrong.

fax modem A modem which communicates with fax machines.

female connector A connector socket.

file A document, program, or other grouping of information stored on a disk.

file allocation table See *FAT*.

file area The portion of the disk used to store files.

file compression utility See *archive utility*.

file extension Characters at the end of a file name generally used to indicate what type of file it is.

file server A computer which maintains and distributes the essential files on a local area network.

file transfer protocol A system of communications that ensures that information going from one computer to another is properly transmitted and understood.

fixed disk See *hard disk*.

flatbed plotter A type of plotter where the paper lies flat and still.

flatbed scanner A scanner in which the scanning of the page is automated.

flight simulator A program that lets you simulate the experience of piloting an airplane.

floating-point unit A special (called a math coprocessor) section of a processor designed specifically to handle complex math calculations quickly. Abbreviated FPU.

floppy disk A magnetic disk in a covering jacket which is used to store information.

floptical A disk drive which reads and writes information magnetically, but uses light to help keep the read/write head on track.

font A design of type in a specific size.

footprint The amount of space that a computer or peripheral takes up on the surface on which it is placed.

foreground Describes the program in a multitasking system to which keyboard input goes.

formatting Preparing a disk so that it can store files.

FPU See *floating-point unit*.

fragmented A condition where the files on a disk are broken up over many noncontiguous clusters.

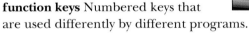

frequency The measurement of rate of waves or cycles.

function keys Numbered keys that are used differently by different programs.

game adapter An expansion board which provides game ports.

game port Connection for a joystick.

GeoWorks An operating environment.

gigabyte 1,024 megabytes.

GND The ground wire in a serial I/O connection.

graphic accelerator A video adapter designed for faster processing of display information.

graphic adapter See *video adapter.*

graphical user interface A system of communicating with a user using images as well as text. Abbreviated GUI.

gray scale The number of different shades of gray that a scanner can interpret.

ground An electrical line used to provide a base voltage necessary to complete a circuit.

GUI See *graphical user interface.*

hammer pin The solenoid device which slams a printer's character arm against the ribbon.

hand scanner A manually operated scanner.

hard disk A disk drive designed to store a large amount of information.

head actuator The device which moves the read/write heads of a hard disk drive.

hertz Cycles per second, a measure of frequency. Abbreviated Hz.

hexadecimal A numbering system which uses a single character to represent each four bits.

high-density Describes floppy disks coated in a way to be able to store more data than double-density disks.

high-level formatting Putting onto a disk the information and indexes that a given operating system needs to be able to keep the disk organized.

horizontal scanning frequency How long it takes the cathode ray tube to fire electrons across one row of screen pixels.

hub The central computer or device in a star configuration local area network.

Hz See *hertz.*

I/O Abbreviation for input/output.

I/O controller An expansion card or set of chips on the motherboard that controls passing information to the I/O ports.

I/O device A device that can exchange information with the computer.

I/O ports Standard ports to which to connect input/output devices.

IBMBIO.COM One of the essential files of PC DOS.

IBMDOS.COM One of the essential files of PC DOS.

icon A little picture used to represent a function or file.

IDE Abbreviation for Integrated Drive Electronics, a standard for communicating between the disk controller and the disk drive.

impact printer A printer which puts ink on the page by slamming character-shaping elements against an inked ribbon, which hits the paper.

index hole A hole cut through the disc and jacket of a 5.25" floppy disk, which allows the computer to find the start of the disk.

init line A line in a parallel I/O connection which is used to reset the device to its initial state.

inkjet printer A non-impact printer which creates images by spraying ink dots onto the paper.

input The process of giving information to the computer, or the information that is given.

installation program A program that sets up your system to be able to run a piece of software.

instruction prefetch Part of a processor that gets commands from memory before they need to be executed.

insulator A material that does not let energy pass through it easily.

interlace A system of refreshing alternate lines of a monitor.

interleave factor How many sectors are skipped for each sector written to or read from an interleaved disk.

interleaving A system of storing data on disk sectors that are not right next to each other, which in some cases can increase disk speed.

internal modem A modem which installs in an expansion slot.

interpreter A program that takes a program written in a programming language and turns it, command by command, into machine language, and then immediately executes the machine language version.

IO.SYS One of the essential files of MS-DOS.

iron oxide A compound used to coat the disc of floppy disks because it holds data easily.

ISA Abbreviation for Industry Standard Architecture, a standard design for the system bus.

joystick An input device that lets you indicate a direction by tilting a stick in that direction.

K See *kilobyte.*

KB See *kilobyte.*

kermit A file transfer protocol.

keyboard An array of buttons that lets the user type information into the computer.

keystroke buffer An area of RAM that stores the keys that have been pressed but that the program has not yet had a chance to process.

kHz See *kilohertz.*

kilobit 1,024 bits.

kilobyte 1,024 bytes. Abbreviated K or KB.

kilohertz A measure of thousands of cycles per second. Abbreviated kHz.

label Text information in a spreadsheet cell.

LAN See *local area network.*

land A flat area on a CD-ROM disk.

laptop computer A computer designed to be easily carried around.

laser printer A non-impact printer in which a laser creates a static image of the page on a rotating drum, which then collects toner on the statically charged portions and delivers it to the page.

LED Abbreviation for light emitting diode. A small electronic device which lights up when electricity flows through it in a given direction.

light pen A wand which, when touched to the screen, can detect which location on the screen it is touching.

line noise Interference and other stray sounds on a communication line.

loading Copying a program from a disk into RAM.

local area network A system of cabling together a number of computers, allowing them to share information. Abbreviated LAN.

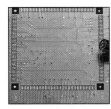

local bus A direct high-speed connection between the CPU, RAM, and other peripherals.

local bus adapter An adapter card which attaches to the local bus.

local bus graphic accelerator A graphic accelerator that attaches to the local bus.

logical operators The different types of comparisons that are possible in binary logic.

low-level formatting Raking out the tracks and marking the sectors on a disk.

machine language The command language that the processor can directly understand.

magneto-optical drives Disk drives which store and read information using a combination of magnetism and light.

mail merge A word processing feature that lets you take information from a series of database records into a fixed form.

male connector A connector with exposed pins or leads that slide into a female connector socket.

matrix A grid.

MB See *megabyte.*

MCA Abbreviation for Micro-Channel Architecture, an IBM-generated standard design for system buses.

mechanical keyboard A keyboard where pressing the key separates electrical contacts.

mechanical mouse A mouse whose movement is measured by the turning of an encoder wheel across electrical contacts.

membrane keyboard A keyboard where pressing the key pushes electrical contacts together.

meg See *megabyte.*

megabit 1,048,576 bits.

megabyte 1,048,576 bytes. Abbreviated M or meg.

millisecond A thousandth of a second.

modem A device that allows computers to communicate with each other over phone lines.

modulate To vary sound, or to adapt. A modem does both in encoding information as sound.

monitor A TV-like information display.

motherboard The printed circuit board where the main electronics of the computer reside.

mouse An input device which is controlled by sliding it across a flat surface.

MS-DOS An operating system produced by Microsoft Corporation.

MSDOS.SYS One of the essential files of MS-DOS.

Multiscan monitor A monitor that can accept and display data at more than one display frequency.

multisession Describes a CD-ROM drive that supports a special directory format which allows information to be added to a disk by special devices designed for that purpose.

multitasking A system of running more than one program on a computer, seemingly simultaneously.

multithreading Running more than one chain of commands in a single program, seemingly simultaneously.

NAND A logical operator that puts out a true (or 1) value if either of the values going in are false (or 0).

nanosecond A billionth of a second.

near letter quality An operating mode of dot-matrix printers which achieves sharper-looking characters by making multiple passes across each line. Abbreviated NLQ.

network interface card An expansion card which allow a computer to hook up to a local area network.

Nike network A nickname for the practice of regularly transferring files from computer to computer on floppy disks.

NLQ See *near letter quality*.

non-impact printer A printer which forms characters without striking the paper.

NOR A logical operator that puts out a true (or 1) value only if both of the values going in are false (or 0).

NOT A logical operator that puts out the opposite value of what is put in.

Novell DOS An operating system that emulates the functions of MS-DOS.

null modem cable A cable that allows you to connect to computer serial ports directly, so it will appear to the computers as if they are connected via a modem.

nybble Half a byte.

OCR Abbreviation for Optical Character Recognition, a system of translating scanned text into a form that the computer can understand as text.

odd parity One of two methods of calculating a parity bit value.

operating environment A program system which provides tools in addition to the ones built into the operating system.

operating system A series of programs designed to handle many of the essential processes of the computer. Abbreviated OS.

optical drives Disk drives which write or read information using light.

optical mouse A mouse where the movement is measured by light bouncing off of a gridded pad under the mouse.

opti-mechanical mouse A mouse where the movement is measured by light passing through slots in a rotating wheel.

optimizer See *defragmenter*.

OR A logical operator that puts out a true (or 1) value if either of the values going in are true (or 1).

OS See *operating system*.

OS/2 A multitasking, multithreading operating system produced by IBM.

output The process of getting information out of a computer, or the information that comes out.

overlay Pieces of a program that can be loaded into and out of memory separately from the main program.

packet A group of characters transferred from one computer to another, including control information.

page description language A printer command language that includes the ability to describe an entire page as groups of objects. Abbreviated PDL.

page printers Printers which print a whole page as a single action, rather than a single character or single line.

paint program A program that lets you draw pictures by setting the colors of pixels.

palette The colors that can be chosen for a computer image.

paper out line A line in a parallel port connection used by printers to announce when they are out of paper.

parallel port A connector that can exchange data with an I/O device eight bits at a time.

parity bit A calculated bit used to check the integrity of a character of data.

partition A group of cylinders of a hard disk that appear to the system to be a single, separate disk drive.

PC See *personal computer.*

PC DOS A version of the DOS operating system produced by IBM.

PDL See *page description language.*

personal computer A small computer designed for a single user. Abbreviated PC.

phase The spacing between two similar waves.

phosphorous A chemical that glows when struck by electrons.

pit A small area dug out of a CD-ROM disk.

pixel A small rectangle which is the smallest possible piece of a graphic image.

platen The cushioned cylinder that paper wraps around in some printers.

platen knob A knob which allowsyou to turn the platen manually.

platters Individual disks of hard disk media.

plotter A type of printer which draws lines on the page with a pen.

pointer A user-controlled screen image which points to things.

POST Abbreviation for Power On Self Test, a series of checks that the computer runs through when turned on to make sure that everything is working okay.

power supply A device inside the computer which regulates and distributes the electricity for the computer's internal components.

PPM Abbreviation for pages per minute, a measure of printer speed.

preemptive multitasking A system of multitasking that does not require the programs to voluntarily processor control on to the next program.

Presentation Manager A user interface system in OS/2.

print head The portion of some printers which slides along the page, putting the characters on the paper.

printer An output device which puts information on paper.

printer driver A small program designed to allow another program to communicate with a specific brand and model of printer.

printer ribbon A long strip of fabric saturated with ink, used in impact printers.

processor A chip which processes commands. See also *central processing unit.*

professional word processing program A word processing program with a full range of functions.

program A list of computer commands designed to perform a specific function.

program file A file that stores a program.

programming language Any of a number of systems for describing commands to the computer.

quick format A method of clearing information from a disk without actually reformatting it.

RAM See *random-access memory.*

RAM disk An area of RAM set aside to store files.

random-access memory Memory chips that store information that can be easily read or written to. Abbreviated RAM.

range the total number of different colors that a video adapter can support.

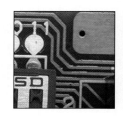

Read-only memory Information storage that cannot be changed by the standard computer. Abbreviated ROM.

read/write head The part of a disk drive that actually reads and writes the information on the disk.

record A single entry of information in a database.

registers Special data storage locations on a processor.

regular-density Describes floppy disks with a coating able to hold the minimum amount of data.

removable hard disk A special sort of hard disk where the platters and some of the mechanism is removable.

repeater A device which can serve as a hub of a local area network.

resolution The density of dots that are used to make up an image.

RI Abbreviation for ring indicator, the line in a serial modem connection used to indicate that the phone is ringing.

ribbon cartridge A plastic casing that holds a printer ribbon.

RISC Abbreviation for Reduced Instruction Set Computing, a processor design philosophy that focuses on being able to handle a few instructions quickly.

ROM See *Read-only memory*.

root directory The first directory on a disk.

RTS Abbreviation for request to send, the line on a serial I/O connection that the computer uses to let the device know that it is ready to accept data.

RX The line in a serial I/O connection on which the device transmits data.

scanner A device which transfers paper images into the computer.

scanning frequency How quickly the electron beam passes across the screen.

screen mode A display format supported by a video adapter, defined by the resolution, the number of colors it supports, and whether it expects information as text or as graphics.

SCSI Abbreviation for Small Computer Standard Interface, a standard for communicating between a controller, disk drives, and other devices.

sector An arc-shaped section of a disk.

sector header An area at the beginning of a sector that contains the sector number.

segment A 64 kilobyte chunk of memory.

select button A printer control button which allows you to take it on-line and off-line.

select input line A line in a parallel I/O connection used by the computer to control whether the device is on-line.

select line A line in a parallel I/O connection used to tell the computer whether the printer is on-line or off-line.

serial port A connector that lets the computer exchange information with an I/O device one bit at a time.

shadow mask A filter inside the cathode ray tube of a color monitor that directs the electron streams toward the proper colors of phosphorous dots.

shadowing Copying the BIOS from ROM to RAM, to make it run faster.

sheet feeder A device which loads individual pieces of paper into a printer.

side The top or bottom of an individual platter or disc in a disk drive.

silicon The primary element of the construction of transistors.

SIMM Abbreviation for Single In-Line Memory Module, a board with RAM chips on it designed to fit into a standard slot.

sneakernet A nickname for the practice of regularly transferring files from computer to computer on floppy disks.

soft-formatting See *high-level formatting*.

solenoid A magnetically controlled two-position electric device.

sound digitizer A device that turns a sound into computer data which can be used to re-create the sound.

space-saver keyboard See *compact keyboard*.

sports simulation A game program designed to represent a popular sport.

spreadsheet A calculation program that lets you lay out numbers and equations on a grid, in a way that makes it easy to change the numbers and recalculate.

star configuration A local area network layout which involves each computer talking directly with a central hub.

start bit A bit sent to indicate the start of a character in a serial communication.

stop bit A bit sent to indicate the end of a character in a serial communication.

stress relief notch Small holes cut out of the edge of a 5.25" floppy disk to prevent warping.

subdirectory A directory which exists as part of another directory.

super VGA A video adapter that goes beyond the VGA standard.

support file A file that a program needs in addition to the program file.

surge protector A device that plugs in between the computer plug and the power socket, that is designed to protect the computer from damage from bad electrical lines.

system area The portion of the disk devoted to organizing the disk structure.

system board See *motherboard*.

system bus The series of electronic wiring and adapter slots that allows the processor to communicate with most peripherals.

system disk A disk that has the operating system on it, and therefore can be used to start the system.

templates Pre-made page designs for word processing or desktop publishing programs.

text mode A mode of display or interface that works without graphics.

thin ethernet A cabling standard for local area networks.

time slicing Dividing the processor time over several different programs, giving each a limited amount of time before moving on to the next program.

toner A fine black powder that takes the place of liquid ink in laser printers.

touch screen A monitor with the built-in ability to detect where on the computer a user's finger is touching.

tower computer A computer designed to stand on the floor, generally next to a desk.

track A single circular path on one side of a disk.

trackball An input device where the user rolls the top of a ball with his hand.

tractor feed A system of pulling paper through a printer, that requires paper with a series of holes along the edges.

transistor A switch-like electronic device that lets electrical current pass through only if a specific charge is applied to it.

triple-spin Describes a CD-ROM drive which spins the disk at three times the standard rate, allowing the information to be read more quickly.

true color Used to describe video adapters that support so large a range of colors that they can display pictures that are indistinguishable from a TV display.

twisted pair-cable A type of cable with pairs of intertwined wires running through it, twisted together.

TX The line in a serial I/O connection on which the computer transmits data.

undelete To recover a deleted file.

uninterruptible power supply A device designed to continue providing power to the computer when the standard electrical supply fails. Abbreviated UPS.

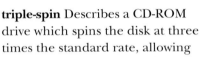

upload To transfer files from your computer to another computer over a modem.

UPS See *uninterruptible power supply*.

variable resistor An electrical device which lets a different amount of power pass through depending where on the device the electrical contact is made.

VDU Video display unit. See *monitor*.

vertical scanning frequency How quickly the monitor can refresh the entire screen.

VGA Abbreviation for Video Graphics Array, a high-quality standard for video adapters.

video adapter A board or set of chips used to process screen information and relay it to the monitor.

virtual disk See *RAM disk*.

virtual machine A set of memory and processes which function as an entire separate computer.

voice recognition A system designed to understand the human voice.

warm boot Reinitializing a computer without turning it off first.

WIMP Abbreviation for Windows, icons, mouse, and pointer. A description of the elements that make up most graphical user interfaces.

window A rectangular area on the screen used to convey information associated with a specific program or function.

Windows A popular operating environment.

wireless network system A local area network where the computers communicate via radio waves instead of via cables.

word processing program A program that lets you create and change reports, letters, and other text documents.

worksheet The document created and edited with a spreadsheet program.

WORM Abbreviation for Write Once/Read Mostly. Describes a disk where information cannot be erased or written over once written.

write-enable notch A hole cut into a 5.25" floppy disk drive, which is used to indicate to the drive that this disk can be written to.

write-protect switch A switch built into a 3.5" floppy disk which lets the disk drive know whether it is okay to write to the disk.

wxmodem A file transfer protocol.

X-axis The line along which side-to-side position is measured.

XGA Abbreviation for Extended Graphics Array, a very high standard for video adapters.

xmodem A file transfer protocol.

XOR A logical operator that puts out a true (or 1) value only if one but not both of the values going in are true (or 1).

Y-axis The line along which front-to-back or vertical position is measured.

ymodem A file transfer protocol.

zmodem A file transfer protocol.

INDEX

S

scandisk.exe, 12
scandisk.ini, 12
scanners, 8, 172-175, 198
scanning frequency, 126, 198
screen mode, 198
screw-attached covers, 30-32
screwdrivers, 26-27
SCSI
    adapter cards, 198
        CD-ROM drives, 110-112
    controllers
        hard disks, 97
        tape drives, 119
sector headers, 198
Sector not found error message, 102
sectors, 198
seek time (hard drives), 96
segments, 198
select buttons, 198
select input line, 198
select line, 198
selecting
    CD-ROM drives, 106-107
    memory, 78
    modems, 150-151
    ports, 57
    printers, 180-181
    video systems, 127
serial ports, 55-56, 61, 198
setting up adapter cards, 42-43
shadow mask, 198
shadowing, 198
sheet feeder, 198
sides, 198
silicon, 198
SIMMs (single in-line memory modules),
   76-77, 83, 198
slider switches, 43
slots for adapter cards, 41
sneakernet, 198
soft formatting, 198
solenoid, 198
Sound Blaster, 136-140, 142
sound boards, 40
sound cards, 9, 136
    configuring software, 143
    installing, 138-141
    see also audio
sound digitizer, 198
space-saver keyboard, 199
speakers, 8, 142-143
speed of hard drives, 96
sports simulation, 199

spreadsheets, 199
ST-506/412 hard disk controller, 97
Standard DMA channel assignments, 42
Standard IRQ settings, 42
star configuration, 199
start bits, 199
static electricity, 27
stop bits, 199
stress relief notch, 199
subdirectories, 199
Super VGA, 124-125, 199
support files, 199
surge protectors, 199
switches (adapter cards), 43
Synchronous communications, 147
SYSEDIT (Windows), 15
system area, 199
system backup
    DOS 6, 18-19
    pre-DOS 6, 22
system bus, 199
system disk, 199
system testing, 35
SYSTEM.INI, 14

T

tape drives, 9, 116
    helical scan, 117
    internal, 118-121
    quarter-inch tape drives, 116-117
    SCSI controllers, 119
templates, 199
testing modems, 155
testing system, 35
text mode, 199
thin ethernet, 199
time slicing, 199
toner cartridges (printers), 186-187, 199
tools, 26-27
touch screen, 199
tower computer, 199
track, 199
trackballs, 199
tractor feed, 199
transistors, 199
triple-spin CD-ROM drives, 199
troubleshooting
    audio, 137
    CD-ROM drives, 113
    communications, 149
    disk drives, 92-93